How to Sell Your House, Condo, Co-op

Other titles of interest to homeowners
published by Consumer Reports Books:

The Mortgage Book by John R. Dorfman
Homeowner's Legal Guide by Cynthia L. Cooper
How to Buy a House, Condo, or Co-op by
Michael C. Thomsett

How to Sell Your House, Condo, Co-op

Amy Sprecher Bly,
Robert W. Bly,
and the Editors of
Consumer Reports Books

CONSUMER REPORTS BOOKS
A Division of Consumers Union
Yonkers, New York

A.S.B.: To Bob and Alex

Copyright © 1993 by Amy Sprecher Bly and Robert W. Bly

Published by Consumers Union of United States, Inc.,
Yonkers, New York 10703.

Library of Congress Cataloging-in-Publication Data
Bly, Amy Sprecher.
    How to sell your house, condo, co-op / Amy Sprecher Bly, Robert W. Bly,
and the editors of Consumer Reports Books.
        p.   cm.
    Includes index.
    ISBN 0-89043-671-1
    1. House selling.   2. Condominiums.   3. Apartment houses,
Cooperative.   4. Real estate business.   I. Bly, Robert W.
II. Consumer Reports Books.   III. Title
HD 1379.B518   1993
333.33'83—dc20   92-40240
                                                                  CIP

Design by GDS / Jeffrey L. Ward
First printing, May 1993
This book is printed on recycled paper.✪
Manufactured in the United States of America

How to Sell Your House, Condo, Co-op is a Consumer Reports Book published by Consumers Union, the nonprofit organization that publishes *Consumer Reports*, the monthly magazine of test reports, product Ratings, and buying guidance. Established in 1936, Consumers Union is chartered under the Not-For-Profit Corporation Law of the State of New York.

The purposes of Consumers Union, as stated in its charter, are to provide consumers with information and counsel on consumer goods and services, to give information on all matters relating to the expenditure of the family income, and to initiate and to cooperate with individual and group efforts seeking to create and maintain decent living standards.

Consumers Union derives its income solely from the sale of *Consumer Reports* and other publications. In addition, expenses of occasional public service efforts may be met, in part, by nonrestrictive, noncommercial contributions, grants, and fees. Consumers Union accepts no advertising or product samples and is not beholden in any way to any commercial interest. Its Ratings and reports are solely for the use of the readers of its publications. Neither the Ratings, nor the reports, nor any Consumers Union publication, including this book, may be used in advertising or for any commercial purpose. Consumers Union will take all steps open to it to prevent such uses of its material, its name, or the name of *Consumer Reports*.

Acknowledgments

We relied on many people to help us put together this book. Thanks especially to Carol Boone, real estate agent with Coldwell Banker Schlott, Alpine/Closter, N.J.; Ron Mariani, real estate broker at Weichert Realtors, Fair Lawn, N.J.; Marc Garfinkle, Esq., Livingston, N.J.; Roger Hauser, Esq., Englewood Cliffs, N.J.; Wayne Kolb, CPA, Montvale, N.J.; Laurene Janik, legal counsel for the National Association of Realtors (NAR); Glen Crellin, economist at NAR; Robert Haley, Certified Auctioneers Institute (CAI); Ann C. Wood, executive vice-president, CAI. Thanks also to Mike Beugnies, Jim Toth, Peter Daly, and Nancy Varettoni. All of them provided information and comments "from the field" that helped make this book much better. To anyone we've left out, our apologies and thanks nonetheless.

Thanks to our agent, Bonita Nelson, who was always there for us, and to our editor, Julie Henderson, for greatly improving the manuscript and keeping it on target.

Most of all, this book certainly could not have been completed without the help of Magnolia Lozano and Amy's mother, Pat Sprecher, for regularly providing baby-sitting services so we could work.

Contents

How to Sell Your House, Condo, Co-Op

Introduction

Fifty-eight million people in the United States own their own homes. According to a 1991 *New York Times* poll, 32 percent of these homeowners want to move. On average, homeowners move every six to seven years for a variety of reasons—a job transfer; a life-style change such as marriage, divorce, or retirement; or the perennial need for more room, status, or amenities.

No matter what the reason, selling a home is a stressful process. It means you must surrender privacy and leisure time, especially if you sell on your own. Your home will be examined, inspected, and criticized by agents and buyers. You will endure constant interruptions and frustrating encounters with prospects. Not only must you keep the house clean and neat to show on short notice, but you must also be pleasant and cooperative with brokers, agents, people who are "just looking," and demanding buyers.

You will be faced with numerous decisions—from deciding whether you want to sell your home yourself or whether you should offer buyer financing, to what price your property should be listed at and how many concessions to make during negotiations. Selling also means hard work. You may have to renovate or make numerous repairs to your home before it goes on the market, and you must keep it in showing condition for many weeks and possibly months. Above all, you have to keep your wits about you during negotiations, and keep a cool head during the bidding process. The list is longer if you undertake the job of selling your home yourself.

Home sellers must also realize that real estate in the 1990s probably will not be the highly profitable investment it once was. The current view is that people must consider homes first as shelter, and only second as investments. But when tax breaks for mortgage interest payments and property taxes are factored in, home owning still has many advantages for most people.

What does all this mean to you, the seller? It means you need to understand the market if you want to sell your home in a reasonable period of time at a fair price. You'll need to know:

- □ what drives demand in your area
- □ how to evaluate market conditions
- □ when is a good time to sell
- □ whom your home will appeal to
- □ what prospective homeowners look for
- □ how to negotiate with buyers

It also means you must price your property reasonably, show it to best advantage, and market it aggressively. If you sell through a real estate agent, you need to choose the right broker and learn to work successfully with him or her.

HOW TO USE THIS BOOK

Everything you need to know about selling your home is covered in this book.

- □ Chapter 1 tells you how to recognize when it is a good time to sell, based on market conditions, the time you bought your home, and your personal situation.

- The financial considerations of a sale, including capital gains, taxes, and possible company reimbursement, are discussed in chapter 2.
- Chapter 3 explains how to set a realistic market price for your home so that it can be sold within a reasonable length of time.
- Chapter 4 helps you evaluate your home's market appeal and the impact of detrimental situations, including serious property defects or community problems.
- Chapter 5 discusses the advantages of fixing up your home prior to putting it on the market—based on the rooms and improvements that make the most impact on buyers, and what you can do to increase the value of your home.
- The advantages and disadvantages of selling your home yourself are covered in chapter 6, which shows you how to protect yourself and your home, market your property, deal professionally with prospects, and qualify buyers. This section also explains other selling options, such as using discount brokers and home sellers' networks.
- Chapter 7 provides information on how to choose a broker and agent, what services you can expect from your agent, what types of listing contracts exist, what should be covered in the listing agreement, the importance of a marketing plan, whether and how to negotiate commissions, and what to do if you are dissatisfied with your agent.
- Chapter 8 offers tips on selling in a buyer's market, including home warranties, incentives to buyers and agents, what to do with hard-to-sell properties, and a list of creative marketing strategies.
- Financing options that may help a buyer purchase your home are covered in chapter 9, which examines how useful such strategies are, what types of homes are the most likely candidates for seller-sponsored financing, and what possible pitfalls there might be for both buyer and seller.
- Chapter 10 deals with the unique considerations facing owners of condos and co-ops, including likely target mar-

kets, and problems with maintenance fees, bylaw restrictions, and co-op approval boards.

☐ When you can't sell your home through more traditional methods, chapter 11 provides alternative strategies, including trading or swapping properties, auctions, and various renting options.

☐ Chapter 12 gives advice on how to handle low offers, and how to negotiate with difficult and demanding buyers.

☐ Chapter 13 looks at contracts and what you need to know before you sign anything. A list of common contingency clauses is provided, along with guidelines on how to protect your interests without jeopardizing the sale.

☐ Chapter 14 explains what happens when the deal is finally concluded, and what you, your real estate agent, and your attorney can do to close successfully.

We wish to emphasize, however, that this book is not intended as a substitute for professional or legal advice. If legal or other professional advice or assistance is required, the services of a competent professional should be sought.

Because careful preparation and advance planning are the keys to a successful sale, we hope that the information in these pages will help you sell your property—alone or with the help of an agent—for maximum profit and with a minimum of frustration and stress.

1

Putting Your Home on the Market

During the 1980s, the median national price for resale houses — which account for 80 percent of residential home-buying transactions — edged up only 4.58 percent a year nationwide, according to the National Association of Realtors. In fact, the median value of homes rose just 5 percent during the decade, after adjusting for inflation.

It was the 1970s that brought the truly big gains in the housing market. During that decade, the real median value of owner-occupied homes soared by 39 percent, and their current-dollar value nearly tripled, from $17,000 to $47,200.

If you didn't buy your home in the 1970s or before, don't despair. Since 1950, housing prices have typically risen about 2 percent per year faster than inflation, which has averaged 5 percent per year. Only during past recessions have home prices not kept pace with the higher prevailing rates of inflation. And while most economists predict that homeowners will build up equity less quickly than they did in the past, the consensus is that housing prices in the 1990s should rise slightly faster than inflation, with only occasional fall-backs.

Traditionally, the housing market has always relied on first-time buyers to keep the chain of home buyers moving. But to move up, people have to be able to sell their current, smaller residences. Yet only 53 percent of those aged 30 to 34 are homeowners, while 80 percent of those 55 to 64 years old own their own homes. As their incomes rise and homes become more affordable, aging baby boomers who couldn't afford homes in the 1980s may increase the demand for homes in the 1990s.

DECIDING TO SELL

When you bought and when you sell can mean the difference between taking a loss or making a profit. It's tough to buy at the top of the market and find yourself selling into the bottom of one. But if you're buying another home, the money you save on that transaction can more than make up for what you "lose" now. In a depressed market, you should probably go ahead and sell, if the following conditions exist:

- □ You have a pressing need—a job change, divorce, or severe financial problems.
- □ You want to move up to a bigger home in the same area, and you expect to make up for what you lose on the sale of your home by paying less for the new home. In fact, if you plan to "trade up," it is wise to make your move sooner rather than later. You don't want to wait out a down market for several years, since that may be how long it takes for the market to recover.
- □ Predictions are that prices in your area will continue to drop or stabilize for some time to come (with no upward trend in sight).
- □ The local economy is uncertain and may get worse before it gets better.
- □ There are proposed construction projects or zoning changes that might have a negative impact on your neighborhood (thereby decreasing property values). In that case, however,

you have an obligation to tell your agent and buyers about the proposed project, to protect yourself from liability in the future.

□ The property you are selling is an estate sale (that is, you inherited it). If you are not going to live in the home, it makes more sense to sell than to have maintenance costs and worries about vandalism, burglaries, or burst pipes.

Under the following conditions, you might want to delay selling into a soft market:

□ You bought your home at market peak and would take a substantial loss if you sold now, especially after broker's commissions, closing costs, and moving expenses are factored in.

□ You bought too recently to have any equity built up in your home, especially after selling and transaction costs are taken into account. By waiting a few years, you may accumulate enough equity to offset those costs.

□ Interest rates are high, making it difficult for you to afford a new home and to find a buyer who can afford yours.

□ You bought your home years ago and have a mortgage with an interest rate that is impossible to match today. You might be better off renovating or adding on. Or you might want to use your older home as a rental investment, especially if you don't need the cash from the sale to buy another home. The annual rental income, minus mortgage payments, maintenance, taxes, and other expenses, might give you a positive cash flow.

□ Population influx into your area is likely within a couple of years because a new company headquarters, leisure or cultural attraction, or retail development is moving into the region, and housing values are expected to rise.

The decision to sell also depends on your personal reasons for moving. In fact, your motivations directly affect how you price and market your home and therefore how quickly you can expect to sell it.

If you don't have to move by a specific date, for example, you have options in terms of pricing and how you negotiate the sale. If you can't get the price you want initially, you can take your home off the market and relist it later. Even in a sluggish housing market, time is on your side. Past history has shown that real estate is cyclical, and you may be able to wait for a rebound and higher prices. Obviously, you should not sell if you are uncertain about your future move, or if your spouse isn't as committed to the idea of selling as you are. Selling without a compelling reason causes all kinds of problems, from not accepting perfectly good offers to antagonizing brokers and buyers by uncooperative or erratic attitudes or behavior.

Uncertainty can even lead to a lawsuit. If you change your mind after accepting an offer from a ready, willing, and able buyer, the broker or the buyer could sue you for the commission or damages.

EVALUATING THE MARKET

Before you decide to sell your home, consider the state of your local housing market, interest rates, and the season. Singly and together, they help determine how successful or unlikely your prospects of selling will be.

The Local Economy and Real Estate Market

Your home's value is clearly linked to your area's economy. If local employment is rising or at least holding steady, people will be able to find work in your area. They may even be attracted to the area because of the availability of jobs. Conversely, a high unemployment rate is bad news for home sellers.

Other signs of a strong local economy are rising incomes, new and flourishing stores and businesses, office vacancy rates below 10 percent, increasing development of commercial and residential buildings, a diversified economic base, and a growing population. Affordable commercial space and attractive residential housing also draw businesses and residents to an area.

If you're uncertain about selling, the condition of the real estate market in your neighborhood may well dictate your decision. Is it sluggish or picking up steam as spring approaches? You may already have an idea of what's going on in your community. If not, it's easy to find out.

Read the Local Newspapers. Real estate markets can vary substantially from one neighborhood to another, even within the same general area. To get an accurate reading of your market, pay close attention to the real estate section of your local newspapers.

Classified ads provide clues to the trend in home prices; phrases such as *price reduced, priced below appraised value,* and *seller wants offer* may signal a troubled market, as do markdowns, high new-home inventory, developer-sponsored discount financing plans, and real estate auctions.

Your newspapers may also provide statistics on housing inventory and the length of time that resale homes stay on the market. In a hot market, houses typically turn over within 60 days. In a poor one, they may take 120 days or longer to sell. If your newspaper doesn't provide "days on market" statistics, a local real estate agent can get that information for you.

There are subtler signs to look for, as well. An increased demand for real estate agents—as announced in ads, signs, and newspaper articles about job opportunities in the field—can indicate a warming market. Conversely, For Sale signs in front of a large number of houses in your community could indicate a troubled local economy and a poor selling climate. The length of time these signs stay up is another indicator of the market's strength or weakness. The quicker homes in your neighborhood get sold, the better the market.

Talk to Real Estate Agents. Let agents and brokers know you're thinking about selling. They can get helpful statistical information for you from their computers, including how many homes are on the market in your area, how those figures compare with previous years, and how close recent sales prices were to asking prices.

You can also ask your local real estate board, agent, or municipal tax office for sales volume figures. Home prices echo volume patterns: when the number of sales goes up from quarter to quarter, so do prices; when volume consistently heads down, prices tend to drop. Keep in mind, however, that rising prices typically lag behind the first signs of an increase in volume by some 12 to 18 months.

Another key factor is the competition in your area. How many homes are for sale on your street? How are they priced? What condition are they in? From a buyer's point of view, how do they compare to your home? How much sales traffic have they generated? The listing agents for the houses should provide this information, especially if you explain that you're thinking of putting your home on the market soon. Good agents know that making contacts and providing information are part of their job to build future business.

Mortgage Interest Rates

A "domino effect" rules in the housing marketplace; home sellers who want to move up to bigger homes need entry-level buyers who can afford their current residences. Without the latter, sellers trying to trade up aren't able to buy, and the health of the entire real estate industry suffers. So, whether you are selling a modest starter home or a mansion, your success depends at least partly on conditions facing first-time buyers. Traditionally, lower interest rates have been the incentive for those buyers to enter the market.

Lower rates (under 10 percent for a 30-year fixed-rate mortgage is considered good) mean renters and those who were previously locked out of the market can buy starter homes. When interest rates rise, mortgage costs increase and home sales decline.

The other good news about low interest rates is that home prices and interest rates generally don't move in the same direction for long. When low interest rates spur buying, prices tend to go up along with the demand.

To find out current mortgage interest rates, check mortgage

company and bank ads and mortgage-rate charts in the local newspapers. Many newspapers publish comparison charts, showing current and previous rates. HSH Associates, a mortgage evaluation firm, publishes a weekly *Mortgage Update* that surveys 2,000 lenders across the country on their mortgage rates. (For more information, contact HSH Associates, 1200 Route 23, Butler, NJ 07405; 201-838-3330.)

Fixed-rate mortgages are the loans preferred by the majority of today's buyers. Traditional fixed-rate mortgages of 30 years or less command about 80 percent of the market, or at least they have done so in the past several years. The reason is that both the economy and demographics have led to more-conservative attitudes toward the assumption of loans and the building of equity. Baby boomers are now in their forties and are concerned with debt, financial security, and planning for the years ahead.

People who expect to stay in their homes for a long time favor fixed-rate loans, which offer the security of the same monthly payment for the life of the loan. Fixed-term rates also command more of the market when interest rates are low and the spread between fixed and adjustable rates lessens.

If you're selling a starter home, however, *adjustable-rate mortgages* (ARMs) may be more popular with first-time buyers. An adjustable-rate mortgage is one in which interest payments change periodically, usually every two or three years, depending on the agreement with the lender. The change is based on interest-rate fluctuations in a specified index. Lenders obviously prefer this type of mortgage over fixed-rate mortgages, and usually offer them with below-market introductory interest rates. Although borrowers with less income may qualify for these types of mortgage loans, their main disadvantage is a serious one: greater financial risk if interest rates should rise in the future.

WHEN TO SELL

Most buyers prefer to move in the spring or summer, after school lets out. With this date in mind, the market traditionally starts to pick up around the middle or end of February. Many home sellers list their homes with agents at this time, hoping to move out by the end of the summer.

To attract the largest number of potential buyers, put your house on the market in late winter or early spring. Spring is also the time of year when houses tend to look their best; trees, plants, and flowers soften harsh lines, open windows let in light and air, and there are more daylight hours to show the house to advantage.

July and August are typically slower months because of vacations and the distractions of summer activities. But the average price of homes sold nationally often increases during the summer because of the number of trade-up homes sold to families who want to move before the school year begins.

After spring, the best time to list your property is in the fall. But in order to sell before the holiday season, you must set your price realistically. The selling season is shorter and there isn't much time to alter your price if it is too high. You may have to wait until the next spring to see interest in your property pick up.

In the past, the most difficult time to sell a home was in November and December, when people are busy with the holidays. But astute home buyers now realize they can often get better buys during the off-peak season, so this is no longer the case. And houses can look more attractive and inviting when they are decorated for the holidays.

Other considerations that may affect your timing include annual festivals or events that attract many visitors to your area. You may want to have your house already listed, with the For Sale sign up, when the busy season arrives, depending on the nature of the event and whether it attracts potential out-of-town buyers.

If you are selling a house in a summer resort area, you'll fare best if you list in the spring or early summer. That's the time of year when people are naturally thinking about vacation and may be willing to pay more if they can get the use of your property for the upcoming season. On the other hand, you may be able to sell your home faster (though not necessarily for the best price) in the early fall, when summer renters are eager to buy, and bargain hunters are out in full force.

ALTERNATIVES TO SELLING

At this point, you may be discouraged about the prospect of selling your home, at least for the immediate future. Or you may prefer to remain where you are, if only you had a bigger kitchen or an extra bedroom. The chief alternative to selling your house is renovation or adding on a room or two.

Besides making your home more attractive and livable for you and your family, you may want to upgrade your residence in the hope of getting a better price when you do sell. Of course, these reasons are not mutually exclusive; you might want to remodel now to make your house suit your immediate needs, while you wait for a better market.

If you do the work yourself, you can generally expect to recoup more than the cost of the project. If you hire professionals to do the work, you may not break even, but your property might sell faster, not only because of the improvements but because of the quality of the job.

Another alternative is to buy the materials yourself through home-improvement centers. These centers provide someone to do the installations and improvements, and you can save about 15 percent as compared with hiring your own contractor.

IMPROVEMENTS THAT PAY OFF

Not surprisingly, kitchens and bathrooms are the remodeling projects that offer the highest return on your investment. Added space, light, and new appliances are the most desirable improvements for a kitchen. Updating a bathroom with new fixtures, wall tile, and flooring helps bring a higher price, too. Adding a half-bath or second bath to a one-bathroom home is always a good idea. Indeed, bathroom remodeling or expansion can return more than 100 percent of the cost when you sell. A second bath for a three-bedroom home can return twice what you have invested in it.

Other projects that return 60 percent of their cost or better are

FINDING THE RIGHT CONTRACTOR

Everyone has heard horror stories about home renovations that went seriously awry when the contractor took months to finish, was incompetent or used poor materials, or simply disappeared in the middle of the job. If you decide to remodel or add on to your existing home, and are looking for a reliable contractor, keep these points in mind:

1. Always ask for references before you engage anyone to work on your home. Check with neighbors, friends, and relatives who have had work done recently. Take a good look at the work first; if you are impressed, get a referral. Ask the contractor referred to you to furnish the names and addresses of other satisfied customers. Visit these people, check the work, and ask questions about the contractor's professionalism and the length of time it took to finish the project. Also check with your local Better Business Bureau to find out if there are any complaints in their files against this particular contractor.

2. If the contractor is using subcontractors—electricians, plumbers, carpenters—make sure he or she carries adequate insurance and workers' compensation insurance.

3. Get at least three estimates from three contractors, and don't necessarily take the lowest bid. If the one you like has presented the highest bid, see if he or she is willing to reduce the price to accommodate you.

4. Draw up a contract with the contractor of your choice, including a full description of the work to be done, start and completion dates, proof of insurance, agreement that the contractor will apply for all necessary permits, and a payment schedule. Never pay all or most of the money up front—a good sum should be withheld until the job is completed to your satisfaction. Make sure you get proof of payment for any subcontractors or materials suppliers.

fireplaces (except in the South), insulation, and new roofing and siding. Replacing windows and doors with energy-efficient models is worthwhile, especially if you are going to stay in your home for a number of years and can reap the benefit of lower energy bills. And a home short on storage space can profit from added shelving, cabinets, and storage systems.

Returns on some improvements vary, depending on the region and the type of house. Low-maintenance vinyl or aluminum siding is valued more in the Northeast than in the West; central air-conditioning brings a higher payback in the South than in the North. Other rules of thumb: Upscale communities offer higher returns on remodeling projects. And a depressed housing market, of course, offers less of a return.

Although home buyers today tend to have smaller families, the three- or four-bedroom house with two and a half baths is expected to retain its appeal. So if your home has two bedrooms, adding a third is a worthwhile investment. Adding a master suite—perhaps by converting two small bedrooms or a family room—might also provide a payback of 75 to 80 percent of the cost. Ideally, such additions should be designed by an architect or an experienced contractor to ensure a well-laid-out floor plan and a good blend with the existing style of your house.

Other remodeling projects that repay their initial cost are improved lighting using high-quality fixtures, or a well-placed skylight in the kitchen or any dark room or hallway. Cosmetic improvements, of course, are essential to a successful sale, especially painting both inside and out in neutral colors. Landscaping makes a big difference if your lawn or outside areas are not particularly attractive. But don't spend more than 5 to 10 percent of your home's value on landscaping, and don't exceed the standard for your neighborhood. Adding a deck or a screened-in porch may or may not be a worthwhile project, depending on the style of your house, the extent of your property, and what features are predominant in the homes in your area.

The one improvement you should not make in most areas, in terms of resale value, is a swimming pool. A pool might be valued in Florida or California, or in a second home in a resort town; in other areas it can actually detract from a property, because it is both a maintenance headache and a danger to children and pets. Other improvements that will probably not pay back their cost are elaborate security systems and automatic sprinkler systems.

Above all, do not overimprove your home to the point where your house costs more than the next most expensive house on the block. In addition, avoid making idiosyncratic or unusual improvements to a home, such as expensive built-ins, wall murals, or a darkroom. They will appeal to only a minority of home buyers, and may actually prevent a sale.

Here are the key points to consider before you forge ahead with remodeling:

□ Rethink any project that will raise your home's value more than 20 percent above similar houses in the neighborhood. It will be difficult to get back the money you put into it, because the less expensive houses on the street will pull its value down, and because most buyers buy location before they buy the house. A well-known real estate dictum says that it's smart to buy the cheapest house in the best neighborhood you can afford, because its value can increase proportionately.

□ Don't remodel one part of your house out of proportion to the rest of it. Expanding the master bedroom to include a sitting room and a large master bath makes much more sense in a large "executive" home than in a small three-bedroom tract house.

□ If you plan to move within 18 months, don't expect to get back your remodeling investment, especially on big projects. Instead, spend less and eliminate the main drawbacks of your home, such as old flooring or appliances, crumbling tiles, or shabby kitchen cabinets. It's better to spend a few thousand dollars to bring an unattractive and inefficient kitchen up to an acceptable level than to spend $20,000 to create a "dream" kitchen that far outshines the rest of the home.

- □ Don't expand your house so much that it looks too big for your lot, or takes up too much valuable yard space. The house may end up looking out of proportion not only to its lot, but to other homes on the street. An extension or swimming pool added to a small lot makes the property less attractive, and many buyers resent the loss of outdoor space.
- □ Carefully consider whether the proposed improvement really will solve the problems with your current house and appeal to most buyers. For example, a family room addition might not make sense if it has no access from the kitchen; remodeling a basement into a recreation area isn't worth the money if it's dark or damp; combining a dining room and kitchen into a larger eat-in kitchen may later become a drawback to buyers who prefer a separate, formal dining room.

2

Considering the Finances

Before you decide to sell your home, you should know how much equity you have in it, and how trading up can defer taxes on the capital gains. These financial aspects will help determine how likely you are to make a profit from the sale and whether you can postpone handing over part of that profit to the government. They can also affect your ability to take on a larger mortgage or provide financing to buyers. If you have only a small amount of equity in your home or expect to lose money when you sell, you will be reluctant to make price reductions or even to pay a full commission to a real estate broker.

EQUITY

Equity is the real market value of your property, minus any existing loans and *liens* (a lien is a monetary encumbrance against property in order to meet an unpaid obligation). To determine the amount of equity you have in your home, you need to know the market value of your property, the principal amount remaining on your mortgage, and the sum of the liabilities against your house, such as home equity loans.

To get an estimate of your home's fair market value, ask several real estate agents to perform a *comparative market analysis* (CMA), or hire an appraiser (see chapter 4). You can find out how much principal you have remaining on your loan by looking at your monthly mortgage statement or by asking your mortgage company or bank for the current figure. Then subtract any principal remaining on your original mortgage amount, plus the principal remaining on any home equity loans or other mortgages against your property, from the estimated market value. The resulting figure is your equity, or how much cash you can expect to receive if you sell your house for the appraised value.

Example: You bought your house for $125,000 six years ago. You put down 20 percent—$25,000—and took out a 10-percent, 15-year mortgage for $100,000. The remaining principal is now $76,328. The house was appraised at $175,000. You have an equity in the house of $98,672 ($175,000 minus $76,328).

CAPITAL GAINS AND TAXES

Closely tied in with equity are *capital gains*. In general, a capital gain is the difference between your *amount realized* on the home (the selling price minus certain deductible expenses related to the costs of selling, such as commissions, legal fees, and any advertising costs paid by you), and the *adjusted cost basis* (the price you originally paid for the home, plus your costs of purchase and any capital improvements).

Capital improvements are expenditures that add to the value of the home, such as an upgraded electrical system, new plumbing, a new front door, a finished basement, or a family room addition. Routine maintenance, such as fixing the roof or interior painting, doesn't count. (Check with your accountant to make sure.)

Such fix-up costs can help reduce your capital gains, however, if you purchase a new principal residence. This is true to the extent that the *adjusted sales price of the old home* (that is, the amount realized minus fix-up expenses) exceeds the cost of the new residence. The work must be done within 90 days of the signing of the sales contract, and payment must be made no later than 30 days after the sale of your home. So save your receipts from painting and any other fix-up repairs.

Example: Using the previous example, assume you sell your home at the appraised price of $175,000. If your selling costs total $10,000, your amount realized is $165,000 ($175,000 − $10,000). If you had purchase costs of $5,000 when you bought the home for $125,000, your adjusted cost basis is $130,000 ($125,000 + $5,000). But if you also spent $25,000 on capital improvements, your adjusted cost basis rises to $155,000 ($125,000 + $5,000 + $25,000).

Your capital gain is determined by subtracting the adjusted cost basis ($155,000) from the amount realized ($165,000). In this case, the capital gain is $10,000. If you now buy a new primary residence for $200,000, make no capital improvements to it, and sell it five years later for $225,000, your capital gain, before deducting sales costs, is $35,000 ($225,000 − $190,000). (Here, as explained below, the cost of the replacement residence—$200,000—is reduced by the deferred gain of $10,000 from the sale of the first home.) Normally, this gain is taxable if you don't buy a new home, so if you're in the 28-percent tax bracket, you will have to pay $9,800 in taxes. Payment of those taxes can be deferred, however, as was the case after the sale of your first home.

Deferring Taxes

If you buy a replacement principal (or primary) residence that costs as much as, or more than, the adjusted sales price of the home you sell, you can "roll over" the gain and postpone paying taxes on it. This tax deferral continues until you buy a home that costs less than the adjusted sales price of the home you last sold, or until you stop owning a home altogether. If you buy a home that costs less than the adjusted sales price of your old home, you must pay taxes on at least a portion of the gain realized. This portion is the lesser of the gain realized, or the difference between the adjusted sales price of your old home and the purchase price of your new one. You may still defer the balance of your gain realized.

Another way to avoid paying the capital gains tax if your new home costs less than the selling price of your old one is to make any major improvements within the two-year period. The costs of the capital improvements are added to the purchase price of your new home, so that your capital gains tax is reduced or completely deferred.

Deferral Rules

This tax-free loan from the government comes with several caveats. You must buy the new, more expensive home within two years of selling your old one. (You can also roll over your gains if you buy a new home first and then sell your current home within two years of buying the new residence.)

The government also requires that you use the deferral rule only once every two years. So you cannot claim the deferral on the sale of more than one house in a two-year period, *unless* you are selling because of a job-related relocation. For example, if you sell house A and buy and sell house B less than two years after the sale of house A, you cannot defer the gain on house B; you can defer the gain on house A only. But if you then buy house C and sell it after two years have elapsed from the sale of house A, you can defer the gain on house C. And if you move three times in two years, selling your home each time because of being relocated or changing jobs, you can claim the deferral in all three cases, provided that in each case your new office is at least 35 miles further from your old residence than was your old office.

In addition, the deferral can be taken only on your principal or primary residence, and on the portion of your home that is a residence. If you rent out part of your house or use a part to operate a business or home office, you cannot defer the gain on that portion.

DETERMINING YOUR PRINCIPAL RESIDENCE

You can take the tax deferral only on a principal or primary residence — not on a secondary residence, such as a vacation home or rental house. A principal residence is the one you physically occupy most of the time. The IRS generally determines primary residence by checking the address on your driver's license, where you vote, where your children attend school, the address on your tax returns, and other such verification.

The capital gains tax obviously affects your decision to sell, if you plan to move to a less expensive home. If you move from an expensive area of the country to a much less expensive one, one option is to rent out your first home temporarily while you rent a place in the new area to see how you like it. But you must sell your home and buy a new one within two years of the sale of your old residence, in order to defer your gains.

Or you can sell your first home and rent a place in the new area for a year or so before deciding to buy. If you decide not to stay in the new location, you still have another year to buy in a higher-priced area and defer your gains from the sale of your home.

Since tax laws are constantly changing, check with your accountant before making decisions regarding improving, selling, or renting your home.

Gain Versus Cash

You are taxed on your home's gain, not on your cash proceeds from the sale of the home. It's easy to confuse the two terms, but they are not the same. Cash proceeds are what remains after subtracting the amount of any mortgages and loans against your home from your sales price minus sales expenses (adjusted sales price).

Example: You bought your first home for $100,000 and sell it for $175,000. Your cost basis for the home is the purchase price ($100,000) plus the purchase expenses of $5,000, plus improvements of $30,000, or $135,000. Your amount realized is the sales price of the home ($175,000) minus sales costs of $15,000, or $160,000. Your *gain* realized is the amount realized minus the cost basis ($160,000 − $135,000), or $25,000.

Your *cash proceeds* on this sale are figured by taking the amount realized and subtracting any remaining mortgages. If you have a mortgage of $70,000, subtract that from the $160,000 amount realized. This represents your equity in your home after you subtract all expenses.

SELLING AT A LOSS

What happens if you lose money on the sale of your home? *Example*: You bought your house for $225,000. You sell it for $200,000. The loss in economic terms is $25,000 (again, assuming no capital improvements were made). If the basis for your home is $225,000 — that is, if you have no prior capital gains rolled over from selling previous homes at a profit—you do not have to worry about paying taxes. You probably cannot claim any tax benefits, either. That's because under current law, the loss incurred from the sale of a residence cannot normally be used as a tax deduction against ordinary income or capital gains. There are a few exceptions to this rule—such as when a seller had a home office, or situations involving the rental of a home prior to selling. Consult a tax adviser for information on the specific tax consequences and benefits involved in these situations.

If you had sold previous homes at a gain and then rolled over those gains when you bought the house you are now selling, the loss on the current house must be deducted from the prior gains. If you realized a gain of $200,000 from selling your other homes,

TRADING DOLLARS

When you bought and when you sell your home can mean the difference between a loss and a profit. As with most long-term investments, the longer you've lived in your home, the more likely it is you will reap a bigger profit owing to inflation and appreciation over the years.

No one wants to buy at the top of the market and then sell into the bottom of one. But if you buy another home, the money you save on that transaction can more than make up for what you "lose" now. Just as the buyer for your home can drive a harder bargain in a soft market, you can do the same when buying *your* next home. The point is to work with the market you must sell into, which means being flexible about price and meeting a buyer's needs. Don't agonize over the money you "could have made" in a better market; instead, focus on the benefits you will reap when you buy.

Similarly, when you sell into a hot market, you get more for your house—but you also pay more for the next home you purchase. Unless you have lived in your home for many years, sell into a bustling market in an expensive area of the country, and buy in a less expensive area, you will probably not be left with much cash in your pocket. But then your cash will be whittled down by your having to pay, in most cases, a great deal in taxes.

But wisdom also dictates that selling and buying a home should not be viewed merely as a dollar transaction; it is a life-style change you are undertaking for other reasons—presumably more important ones.

in effect you subtract the current loss of $25,000 to reach a taxable gain of $175,000.

THE 55-OR-OLDER EXCLUSION

The rollover of capital gains does not continue indefinitely; the gain eventually has to be reported to the IRS when you sell your home and fail to buy a more expensive replacement residence. If, however, you are 55 years or older when you sell, you can qualify for a one-time tax exclusion of up to $125,000 on any capital gains realized from the sale of the home.

To take the exclusion, you must have owned and used the property as your principal residence for at least three of the five years preceding the date of sale. A husband and wife can take only one $125,000 exclusion. If the home is jointly owned by you and your spouse, and you file a joint return for the year in which you sell the home, you may take the exclusion. However, one of you must be 55 years old when the home is sold (and that spouse must satisfy the ownership and use tests).

If you use part of your home as an office, and claim it as a deduction, you cannot take advantage of this once-in-a-lifetime exclusion for that portion of the home. This ruling can substantially reduce the advantages of the $125,000 exclusion, and can cost you more in taxes than you had realized in savings from year to year.

If you do not claim your home office as a deduction for more than two years out of the five years preceding the date of sale, however, you will be entitled to the benefits of the $125,000 exclusion for all your gain from the sale.

Consult your accountant or legal adviser if you have any doubts about your eligibility for this important tax break.

SELL FIRST, BUY LATER

In a buyer's market, sellers are strongly advised not to buy until they sell their old residence. Even if you think you may have a buyer, are confident your house is easy to sell, or have found the perfect house at the best price and don't want to lose it, it's best not to buy until you've sold your old home.

Admittedly, it's difficult to refrain from purchasing a superior home at a good price, but keep in mind that you will probably be able to find a similar property at the same price later on. Even if you think you have a serious buyer for your property, wait until after the contract is signed before committing yourself to the expenses of a new home. More real estate transactions fall through in a soft market, and you don't want to have to pay two mortgages, as well as two sets of property taxes and double maintenance costs. Furthermore, owning two homes will make you desperate to sell the older property, and you will be in a weak negotiating position if an interested buyer does make an offer.

The timing of buying and selling properties is never exact, though, and there are situations that may call for some creative thinking and financing. For example, if you absolutely must have a house and don't want to lose it, and you have an interested buyer for yours, ask the buyer for a lender's commitment letter that demonstrates he or she is a good candidate for a mortgage. This does not guarantee a sale, of course, but it can give you some confidence that the sale will eventually go through.

There are other options if you absolutely must move, whether because of a job transfer, a divorce, or some other emergency, and you need the money from the sale of your current home in order to buy a new property. These options are as follows:

Take Out a Bridge Loan. This type of loan allows buyers to tap the equity in their old home to use toward buying a new one. The equity is used as collateral against the loan, which gives you funds to make a down payment and perhaps pay closing costs. These loans are typically short-term, however, usually for less than a year. You are typically charged a loan fee of 1 percent of the loan amount, and may have to pay additional fees to cover the bank's appraisal, credit, and title reports. These additional fees can range from $500 to $1,000, depending on the price of the home.

Most lenders won't lend more than 75 percent of the value of the home minus any liens, including the original mortgage.

Example: You own a home appraised at $200,000. You have a $125,000 mortgage on the property. You've found your ideal trade-up house, but you've just put the old one on the market. You may be able to get a bridge loan of $25,000 (.75 × $200,000 = $150,000 − 125,000 = $25,000).

Some banks allow the borrower to pay interest only during the term of the loan, with the principal due at the end of the term or when the house is sold. Or the borrower might not have to pay anything until the old home is sold.

Insert a Contingency Clause in the Sales Contract.   If the owner or builder agrees, you could insert a contingency clause stating that the sale depends on your selling the property within a specified time, perhaps for a specified sum. For obvious reasons, this clause is highly unpopular, and makes you a much less desirable buyer.

Rent Out or Refinance Your Old House.   A rental will bring you income, but the rent you receive may not cover your monthly mortgage payments, let alone taxes and maintenance costs. Also, you may need the cash from the sale of your old house to buy the new one.

Another way to use your equity in the old home is to refinance your original mortgage for a higher amount, assuming your home has risen in value over the years.

Example: You bought your house for $150,000, taking out a mortgage for $120,000 (80 percent of its appraised value). The home has since appreciated to $200,000, so now you can get a new mortgage loan for 80 percent of its *new* value, or $160,000. Using the $160,000, you can pay off the balance of your mortgage ($100,000) and have $60,000 remaining to use toward your new home.

But there are disadvantages as well, including having to pay closing costs and a new, higher mortgage on the first house. You have the headache of finding good tenants for the old home as well.

It may also be more difficult to sell your house with a tenant in residence. On the plus side, you may be able to take deductions for mortgage interest and property taxes, refinancing costs, repairs, insurance, agent fees, depreciation, and all home maintenance and utilities costs, from cleaning carpets to paving a driveway. If you rent out half of a two-family house, you can take deductions for half of all such costs related to ownership of your home. Check with your accountant before you rent.

Occasionally, you may find developers or builders who are willing to purchase your old house if you purchase one of their new homes. This is a fairly new type of home financing, and is found in areas of the country where home sales are especially sluggish. If you are interested, check the real estate section of your local newspapers, or ask your real estate agent or broker for more information.

COMPANY RELOCATIONS

If you have to sell your home because of a job transfer, the process will probably be much easier. Most large companies offer some kind of selling assistance to their employees, ranging from paying the broker's commission to purchasing the home outright.

For high-level executives, a corporation may pay a large part of their selling and moving costs. Because companies tend to build flexibility into their relocation policies, especially where valued employees are concerned, it may pay for you to request more than the standard moving package—but ask for the arrangement in writing.

Here are some of the many possible advantages of company relocation assistance:

Payment of Closing Costs and the Broker's Commission. Although many companies pay these costs, there may be a cap on how high the commission can go (6 percent is fairly standard). But some companies also pay you a bonus if you sell your home yourself, because it saves them the time and trouble of doing so. However, weigh the extra cash against the loss of time and the work you will have to devote to marketing and showing your home, especially in a slow market. (You may be under pressure to find a new house, move your family, and start a new job, all within a short period.)

A word of warning: If you sell your home privately through a broker (instead of through your company's relocation agency), and your employer pays the broker's commission and legal fees, you owe taxes on those payments—even if your house sells at a loss. On a $200,000 home, that could add $15,000 to your taxable income. If your home is sold through a relocation agency hired by your employer, the employer pays the fees and you have no tax liability.

Purchase of Your Present Property. Companies know that most transferees need the equity from the sale of their home to buy a new one and can't afford to wait months for a buyer. Under these circumstances, your employer may consent to buy your home from you or arrange for a third party to do so.

An employer is supposed to pay the fair market value of a home—defined as the highest price a willing buyer would pay and the lowest price a willing seller would accept. In a soft market, however, companies tend to be conservative in their estimates.

The problem is that determining fair market value in an uncertain economy isn't easy, especially when there are few buyers. Naturally, your employer wants to resell your property as quickly as possible, because every day it sits in inventory, the company is losing money on its investment. The bottom line, then, is that the company's "fair market value" price may be much lower than you expected.

If the company offer seems low, you can probably defer accepting it for about three months. Meanwhile, you can list the home with a broker or try to sell the house yourself. If you don't find a buyer on your own, you can accept your employer's offer later. If you go this route, be sure to add a corporate rider to your listing contract with a broker. This rider gives you the right to back out of the listing agreement in order to accept your company's offer, and without having to pay the broker any commission.

If your company does buy the home, it probably will spend money fixing it up so that it will sell quickly and at a better price. Corporate-owned homes on the market generally have a good reputation in terms of overall condition and price because corporations, unlike individual owners, don't have an emotional investment in the properties. Selling the home is strictly a business proposition—one that becomes more urgent with each day the company pays for maintenance, taxes, utility bills, insurance, security, and repairs.

Payment for Capital Improvements.   Often, companies reimburse the employee who makes costly improvements just prior to putting the house on the market. If you've recently spent $8,000 on new siding for your house, for example, ask the relocation manager if the company will reimburse you for the expense. Your employer may offer to pay for part of the cost, if not all. Or the company might add the cost of the improvement to its estimate of your home's market value.

Payment of Moving Costs.   Companies frequently pay moving costs, including the packing and shipping of household goods, which typically run between $5,000 and $10,000. Check with your company's personnel department to see if you qualify for such a reimbursement.

Unexpected-Profit Protection

The option of having your company sell your house for you is a big relief when the market is slow, but there is always the possibility that the property will sell for *more* than your employer paid you for it. To protect yourself against this eventuality, try to negotiate beforehand for unexpected-profit protection. Under this arrangement, your employer agrees to pay the difference if the company receives a higher price for the home than was paid to you. Of course, if your employer or any third-party company invests money in fixing up your home, those costs are deducted from the sum due you.

More than likely, however, the company will sell your home at a loss. Most employers prefer to make a quick sale, even at a modest loss, than continue to pay high monthly carrying costs.

3

Evaluating Your Home's Sales Potential

You now may have decided to sell your home, and are prepared to work hard at marketing it successfully. But first you need to know whether it will appeal to prospective buyers, how well it meets buyer preferences, and which features may increase or decrease its value. This information will also help you price your home fairly.

WHAT SELLS A HOME

The average first-time buyer may be uncertain about what he or she really wants in a home, but there are a number of basic factors that influence every sale. They are location, size, age, architectural style, condition and layout, amenities, sense of privacy, and zoning.

Location

Location is the major factor that determines your home's worth. The more desirable the location, the higher the market value and the more appeal the house has to buyers, who think of its resale possibilities. Good neighborhoods always retain their value, even in a soft market.

All things being equal, buyers are investing in the address, and are willing to pay more to live in a better town or section of town. For that reason, a smaller house in an upscale community may be more appealing than a larger house in a less prestigious area. Buyers put a high premium on varied community activities, good schools, and other services provided by prosperous towns.

How does your town, city, or district compare with the surrounding areas within, say, a five-mile radius? Consider the following factors when assessing your town's desirability:

Appearance, Size, and Condition of Homes.   Ideally, your area should compare favorably with other parts of town. Is it more or less residential? Is it older or newer? (Newer areas are usually more desirable, unless the older areas consist of stately, well-kept homes.) Are the houses and lots larger? Is the adjoining town poorer or wealthier?

Appearance of Street and Neighborhood.   Since few houses stand in isolation, yours will look better to buyers if nearby homes and yards are attractive and well maintained. Houses in cul-de-sacs and at low-traffic cross-streets are more desirable than houses near busy main roads. Also, many buyers do not look favorably on a house on a corner lot if it means maintaining a long stretch of sidewalk.

Percentage of Owners Versus Renters.   Owners are perceived as better caretakers of their own property. Since they pay property taxes, owners also have a higher stake in making sure they get good services for their money. Moreover, owners presumably have more interest in maintaining or improving their town's image, since property values are directly affected by a town's appearance, level of services, degree of residential versus commercial development, and quality of facilities.

Residents' General Income Level.   Higher overall income implies that residents have the desire and ability to pay for services and amenities that increase a town's reputation. High-income residents usually want their town to reflect their success and status.

Crime Rate.   Obviously, a low or nonexistent crime rate reflects well on the area and neighborhood. It also indicates a high level of police protection and security.

Quality of the School System.   The value of a good school system cannot be overstated. For many buyers, this is the most important factor in deciding where to live. They typically look at the facilities, the student-teacher ratio, class sizes, test scores, types of special programs, and how many students go on to higher education. So if residents tend to approve school budgets and encourage new programs, emphasize that fact to potential buyers and real estate agents.

Population Growth Patterns.   A growing town with plenty of employment opportunities attracts more residents and more services, which in turn means more potential buyers. Demographics, especially such factors as age, family size, and educational background of residents, also affect your town's desirability and real estate prices. For example, an area with many families is likely to have better schools and bigger homes than an area that attracts mostly senior citizens.

Availability and Quality of Health Care.   Access to high-quality health care is important to both families and an aging population. A prosperous residential area and town will have many professionals servicing the population; similarly, well-established hospitals and nursing facilities are likely to be nearby.

Quality of the Environment.   Buyers want and expect unpolluted water and air, quiet streets, and clean public areas, as well as distance from any industrial complexes, power lines, or toxic waste dumps.

Availability of Public Services.   Police and fire departments, good library facilities, and year-round community activities are all important. The greater the level of funding, size of facilities and staff, and variety and frequency of programs, the more appealing to buyers.

Sanitation and Recycling Services.   The availability and cost of such services can make residents' lives easier or more difficult. Many buyers prefer towns that provide municipal services out of residents' taxes rather than forcing residents to hire their own private services.

Convenience to Transportation, Including Bus, Rail, and Highway Systems.   Access to public transportation is especially important in urban areas where many residents may not have cars. In suburban areas, people who commute to jobs in cities look for adequate highways and reliable train service.

Proximity and Variety of Cultural and Recreational Facilities. Again, the more options the better, especially in suburban areas where residents demand and expect a wide choice of services. In rural or resort areas, a greater premium is placed on the proximity of outdoor recreational facilities, such as ski centers, swimming and boating areas, and so forth. Of course, if your home is located near a beach, lake, golf course, or park, that will increase its value.

Tax Levels as Compared to Other Nearby Communities. Naturally, buyers prefer lower tax bills, because they know taxes are likely to rise rather than decrease. A town with generally high taxes clearly must offer superior educational facilities and recreational attractions as compensation.

Community Spirit. A town that gives the impression of being a real community, where people work together to improve resources and programs, or where citizens are politically active, is high on most buyers' lists. Many prospective buyers, especially those coming from an impersonal urban environment, are looking for a friendly and helpful community with plenty of town-sponsored social activities.

NEW CONSTRUCTION IN YOUR NEIGHBORHOOD?

Competitive housing developments near your home may be an advantage or a disadvantage, depending on several factors. For one, it may make it harder to sell an older residence. Many buyers prefer new homes because they look pristine and unused and feature state-of-the-art appliances and systems, and because developers may offer custom features and tempting financing arrangements.

On the other hand, a new upscale development in your neighborhood can increase the value of your home—especially if your home is perceived as being a part of the new development area.

A local broker can be helpful in this situation and can tell you how the new construction may affect home prices in your neighborhood.

If you think your town qualifies, make a point of stressing to buyers all the various activities and programs available to them, including an active PTA, town parades, a town green or park, theater groups, adult education classes at the local high school, library programs, teen or senior-citizen centers, or any sports facilities that are well maintained and frequently used. Mention any zoning codes that enhance the appearance of the town, such as bans against parking commercial vehicles in driveways, or other such restrictions.

House Size

The majority of buyers—with the exception of single people and some retired couples—want bigger homes. Homes on lots large enough to allow for expansion also attract prospects.

Both the number of rooms in your house and their size have a direct bearing on the home's salability and price. Most buyers are looking for at least 2,000 square feet; 3,000 square feet and more are preferred for trade-up and executive-style homes. (For comparison purposes, the standard three-bedroom, one-and-a-half-bath Colonial with no extra rooms has around 1,500 square feet.) Of course, buyers may have more modest expectations in urban areas such as New York City and Chicago, where space is at a premium.

Most buyers want *at least* three bedrooms and one and a half baths. Move-up buyers want a gourmet-style kitchen, a fourth and sometimes a fifth bedroom, a master suite with a master bath and large closets, and a family room. Homes with only one bath or two bedrooms—even if the rooms are large—are harder to sell.

Most prospective home buyers also prefer these features:

A Paved Driveway. Gravel driveways are hard to maintain, are apt to be messy, and are a distinct disadvantage for children who may want to ride their bikes or play basketball in that area.

A View. A year-round view—one that is not blocked during three seasons by leafy trees—is always a strong selling feature. But buyers may not be willing to pay a large premium for the view alone, unless it is a spectacular vista of river, ocean, mountains, or countryside.

A Large Entranceway or Foyer, with Good Closet Space. Buyers want a large, formal space in which to welcome visitors. A cathedral ceiling, skylights, or a tile or marble floor will make the entry more impressive and more appealing to buyers.

A Mudroom by the Back Door, with Space to Store Boots, Umbrellas, and Coats.   Often built into older homes, a mudroom is a convenient place to dress and undress small children for the outdoors.

A Pantry Room or Closet off the Kitchen.   A separate space for storing groceries, dishes, pots and pans, brooms, and gadgets is always appreciated by buyers.

A Laundry Room in a Location Other Than the Basement.   Most buyers prefer a laundry room on the first floor, off the kitchen, or on the second floor, near the main bath or bedrooms. These locations are more convenient to other work areas or the source of dirty laundry. It also eliminates trips up and down a flight of stairs to the basement.

A Walk-Up Attic.   Attic space is valued because it's useful for storage, and it's often convertible into extra living space. Pull-down stairs are more acceptable than an opening in a hall or bedroom ceiling.

An Attached Garage.   Garages built under a house are not as attractive as those attached to one side, if only because of the danger of carbon monoxide rising to the room above. Also, the driveways of garages under a house tend to be steep and difficult to use in the winter. A detached garage is not as desirable as an attached one. Two-car garages, preferably with storage space, are especially popular.

Age

Many buyers prefer newer houses, because they anticipate fewer repairs or problems in a more modern building. In addition, a newer home often has a modern kitchen, a separate breakfast area, a large family room with fireplace, a master bedroom suite, multiple bathrooms, and a master bath, sometimes with a whirlpool tub or sauna. Appliances are more up-to-date, insulation is better, and there may be extra features, such as a security or intercom system, or central air-conditioning and a central vacuum system. Moreover, the wiring, plumbing, and heating and cooling systems are more efficient, sometimes safer, and less likely to need replacing or repairing over a long period of time.

Of course, many buyers prefer older homes for their character, charm, and quality of workmanship and materials. "Older" in this case can range from 20 years to hundreds of years. Houses more than 60 or 70 years old appeal to a smaller group of buyers, often to people who love to restore and take care of such homes. Well-kept historic houses can command a premium price from that segment of the marketplace.

A large number of people prefer homes built 30, 40, or 50 years ago, because the overall quality of construction is generally superior. Older homes often have plaster walls, hardwood floors, moldings, solid wood doors, high ceilings, and working fireplaces. The wood used was heavier and the interior designs generally more decorative. On the down side, the plumbing and electrical systems may not be as adequate, garage space is probably limited, and bathrooms tend to be small.

New construction is sometimes perceived as shoddy and based on a formula. Builders may have cut corners in mass-produced homes in order to put them up faster and keep prices down. Development homes built in the sixties, seventies, and eighties may have plywood subflooring under the carpeting, fiberboard instead of plywood over the framing, thin walls, boxy rooms, stock or laminated kitchen cabinets (instead of wood), and low-quality windows.

There also may be fewer windows than in older homes, and the doors may be made of interior hollow-core material instead of solid wood. Floor and wall tiles in kitchens and bathrooms may seem thinner. Faucet fixtures, door trims, and moldings and designs are not as distinctive as in older homes. And 15- to 25-year-old homes often lack architectural interest.

Architectural Style

When it comes to architecture, the conventional gets sold first. This means house styles that are standard for the area and predominate in the neighborhood sell before more exotic or unusual types of homes. A contemporary on a street of Colonials is at a distinct disadvantage, as are octagon-shaped homes, oriental-style houses, and 1950s "moderns" (low, ranch-style homes with gently pitched roofs, angular walls of glass windows, colorful exterior walls, carports, high horizontal windows, and small closets).

Of course, the region in which you live dictates tastes as well. Log homes may be sought after in rural New England or the West. Colonials, Tudors, ranches, and split levels are popular in the Northeast, while Spanish or Mediterranean styles are preferred in the Southwest. In the West, buyers prefer ranches with glass doors, patios, and lots of privacy. In the Northwest, buyers like redwood or cedar contemporaries.

Another point to keep in mind: If your house lacks a desirable architectural feature common to most of the other homes on your street—a front porch, a backyard deck, or a garage—you may have more difficulty selling it. You need to compensate by setting a lower price for your home than the other houses would normally bring.

Condition and Layout

The condition of your home has a direct bearing on its price and on how quickly it sells. Condition encompasses both how well the property has been maintained and the layout or design of the rooms. A house whose front entrance is on the side or back, for example, or one that lacks a dining room, is divided into tiny rooms, or has a kitchen on the second floor, suffers some loss in value over comparable houses without such strange design elements.

Homes generally fall into three basic categories:

1. Homes that are in *move-in* or mint condition ("creampuffs" in real estate parlance) have been lovingly cared for by their owners and present virtually no need for any cosmetic or

repair work. They go for more money and move quickly, even in a buyer's market, when prospective homeowners can afford to be picky.

2. Homes in *average* condition typically need some repair work and a general cosmetic clean-up. They may need a coat of paint inside and out, repair of leaky faucets or loose doorknobs, a few windows replaced, the bathtub regrouted, the lawn reseeded, or a new roof or heating system installed.

3. *Fixer-uppers* or *handyman specials* need major work in many areas. In addition to needing a new roof or extensive plumbing repairs, these homes may have cracked walls, crumbling front steps, peeling paint, ancient appliances, a shaky garage or outbuildings, or decrepit bathroom fixtures. You must either make extensive and expensive repairs to sell a house of this type, or ask a substantially below-market price for it.

Handyman specials are especially hard to sell when the market is slow and buyers can get good prices on houses that don't require such costly repairs. So it generally pays to put money into a house in poor condition, no matter what the market.

In a seller's market, creampuffs and even average homes sell quickly. So spending a great deal of money on fixing up your fair-to-good-condition home probably won't pay back the investment. In such a market, cash-limited buyers would rather pay less up front and put the money into the home later themselves.

The more sluggish the market, the more you must repair the major flaws in a home. In a buyer's market, prospective home buyers will look suspiciously at a leaky roof, an old-fashioned heating system, evidence of water problems in the basement, visible cracks in the foundation, or inadequate outlets and electrical service.

The design of a home should allow for a smooth traffic flow from room to room; it should have convenient "routes" to each area without the necessity of trekking through other rooms. Ideally, the bedrooms and living room should be self-contained and private. The dining room and family room should be close to the kitchen, and the downstairs bath or lavatory should be located off a hallway, back entrance, or entry foyer. The upstairs bathroom should be convenient to the bedrooms and not visible from the bottom of the stairs, if possible. Many buyers also prefer a private entry that does not allow a direct view into the living room, kitchen, or family room.

Amenities

A home with special features always appeals to buyers, but some extras count more than others. The following amenities are the ones most frequently preferred in surveys of new-home buyers:

- two and one-half baths (or more), with a half-bath on the ground floor
- a master bedroom suite with bath
- central air-conditioning (except in northern areas)
- one or more fireplaces (except in the South)
- a large entry foyer
- lots of storage space
- a modern, bright kitchen
- a family room or "great room"
- a two-car garage (or bigger)

Don't rush out and hire a contractor to add a family room and more closets to your house. As previously mentioned, the investment in such projects usually doesn't pay back all of the costs. But there are *inexpensive* things you can do to increase the appeal of your residence in line with buyers' desires.

For example, installing closet storage systems will make your closets look roomier and help to organize space that is often wasted. Since closet storage systems have designated spaces for every item of clothing and footwear, they also simplify the task of keeping closets neat for showings.

WHAT BUYERS LOOK FOR IN CONDOS AND CO-OPS

Home buyers shopping for a condo or co-op apartment often have the same preferences as single-family home buyers. Large rooms, well-equipped kitchens, adequate bathrooms, and lots of closet space are high on apartment-seekers' lists.

But there are additional amenities, peculiar to largely urban condo and co-op living, that are sought after by most buyers:

Fireplace. A working fireplace is definitely a plus. Even if it doesn't work, or the home buyer is indifferent to a roaring fire on a cold night, a fireplace serves as a focal point of the living room and adds interest and distinction to the apartment.

Sun. Windows that face south and let in the sun are especially valued in an urban environment. Condo or co-op sellers who possess sun-filled apartments should make sure the windows are kept spotlessly clean, and that any drapes, curtains, or shutters are kept pulled back.

Good Layout. The preferred layout for condos and co-ops usually includes a hallway separating the bedrooms from the living room, dining area, and kitchen. This design ensures privacy, cuts down on noise, and provides better traffic flow.

Desirable Floor. In large buildings, buyers usually prefer to be situated on a middle floor rather than on a very low or high one. Some look for high floors with views, although these apartments are at a disadvantage if the elevator should break down or the electricity is shut off for some reason. Top-floor apartments are often subject to roof leaks. Lower-floor apartments may be affected by street noises, but they do have the advantage of a quicker entry or exit from the building. Garden apartments appeal to many who want a backyard area, but some buyers fear security problems. A well-kept garden, however, can attract many buyers to this type of apartment.

Good Management.   All buyers look for a financially stable, well-run building that reflects an active, responsible board of directors and management company, plus an available, hard-working superintendent. If you can honestly boast of such a combination in your condo or co-op, include that information in your fact sheet and make sure all prospective buyers are aware of this important feature.

If you use your garage mostly for storage, clear it out so that buyers can see there's actually room for a car. Install hooks and shelves or bins to hold items. Your garage will look more spacious and cleaner and give the impression that maintaining your home and yard is easy to do.

If your home lacks a foyer, you might be able to install a partition inside your front door to create the impression of one. Other tricks that give the illusion of an entryway are a different type of flooring (tile or marble, for instance), a raised ceiling with a recessed light or other attractive light fixture, a skylight, a different shade of paint or wall covering on a side wall inside the front door, even careful furniture and plant placement. You might use a folding screen, a sideboard, a wall unit, or an open bookcase filled with books and plants as a divider to set off the living space. A mirror, framed prints, and a small loveseat or bench against a near wall can also help define a foyer.

Another, albeit more costly, possibility is to build an outside entry in front of your current front door. Depending on your home's style, this kind of addition can provide a "cold lock" space that helps maintain a more even temperature inside your home, besides providing a private entryway to greet visitors.

Sense of Privacy

A sense of privacy about a house doesn't necessarily mean a large secluded yard or elaborately planted grounds. But it does mean grounds that boast an attractive, well-maintained fence or thick hedge, one that allows you to use your yard without every move being visible to neighbors. You and your neighbor might be best friends who frequently communicate from one yard to the other, but a prospective buyer may not feel the way you do. An outdoor space that's too open and exposed can lessen interest in a home, and a well-planted, fairly private garden can be the feature that clinches a sale. Trees and thick bushes also block out street noise, and smart landscaping using vines and plantings can soften the hard look of a fence and make a yard appear greener and lusher.

Before installing a barrier fence or hedge, be sure it matches or blends in with the style of the house and any existing landscaping. Also check to make sure the fence is on your property and not on your neighbor's. Finally, ask your town's building inspector about any town restrictions that may apply on the height or type of fence you want to install.

Zoning

Your home's market value is also affected by zoning laws and regulations. A house in an area zoned for commercial businesses, for example, might have its "highest and best use" as professional offices or conversion into a commercial property. A large single-family dwelling in a neighborhood zoned for two-family houses is in a similar situation. If this is your problem, you may be able to obtain a higher price and sell faster if you seek out investors willing to convert your property, or you may want to do the conversion yourself.

If, on the other hand, your house sits on several acres and zoning laws allow a subdivision, you may be able to interest developers in the property or subdivide the land yourself and sell it as several parcels.

Of course, a home has a high value if the zoning and deed restrictions in the area specify large lot sizes and dictate residential-only use. In the interest of preserving the historic character and charm of a neighborhood, some towns even regulate the types of additions and renovations that can be made to a home, including the types of materials that can be used on the exterior. Such restrictions may seem onerous, but they often preserve the beauty, quiet, and natural surroundings that may make your house and neighborhood special and desirable to buyers.

Sometimes houses have legal encumbrances that make them harder to sell. These include the following:

- ☐ An *easement* grants a right to third parties to use a portion of your property for a specified purpose, forever. Easements can include a right-of-way that allows the local utility company to run a power line through your yard, or a driveway that cuts through your property and provides the only access to and from a neighbor's house. Easements cannot generally be removed, nor do they necessarily devalue the property. Some, such as a utility box that contains underground utilities for several homes, are considered advantages.

- ☐ *Encroachment* of a building on your property onto an adjoining property. This could be an addition to a garage that overlaps the boundary line between your land and your neighbor's. The construction may have been unintentional, but once it is discovered, it can result in your having to remove the offending structure. If a neighbor has wrongfully built onto your property, the encroachment will likely be discovered during the buyer's title survey search. If you are aware of the problem, try to resolve it yourself before listing your house. This is important, because most contracts allow buyers to back out of the transaction if undisclosed title problems appear that can't be resolved.

- ☐ *Shared property*, such as driveways or fences.

CONSULT WITH THE EXPERTS

If you find it difficult to be objective about your home's short-comings (as most home sellers do), consider hiring an architect or interior designer for suggestions on some simple improvements that can make a big difference to buyers. The architect should spend a couple of hours looking at your house to develop ideas that will bring it up to par with the other houses in your neighborhood or improve it even further. Agree beforehand on the maximum amount of hours that the project requires.

An architect concentrates on exterior improvements and major interior changes, while designers are concerned primarily with colors, wall coverings, window coverings, interior materials (such as substituting ceramic tile for vinyl flooring, or oak cabinets for metal ones), fixtures, and furniture arrangements. Perhaps stripping off stained or torn wallpaper in the bathroom or bedroom and painting the rooms off-white will make your home appear more spacious and airy. Removing heavy drapes in the living room should allow more light to penetrate, and some lush plants strategically placed can attract the eye and enhance the shape of the room. Installing some latticework to enclose the front porch, adding moldings around doorways and under ceilings, or putting a skylight in a dark hallway may be just the touch your house needs to make it stand out from the competition.

- A *lien* against the property by a creditor, usually a contractor who was never paid, for whatever reason.
- *Deed restrictions*, which may limit the size of the house, swimming pools, tennis courts, fences, and other improvements.

DISCLOSURE LAWS

"Let the buyer beware" is no longer the rule in real estate trans-actions. As the seller, you have a responsibility to reveal defects in your property to prospective buyers (and agents), if only to avoid future lawsuits and liability (see chapter 7).

The disclosure issue is a controversial one, and is still being worked out by individual states. Some states, such as California, Maine, and Virginia, have laws requiring sellers to disclose any problems with their properties. Other states, including Illinois and Washington, require seller disclosure for all "material factors" that affect the value or desirability of a property. In these states, the sales agent cannot be held liable for information provided by the seller, unless the agent has reason to believe it is not true. For example, if the agent sees water stains on the basement walls and you claim the basement was never flooded, the agent then has reason to doubt you. If the agent believes you are knowingly con-cealing defects, he or she can either refuse the listing or caution buyers personally about the suspected problem. At this writing, a number of other states—including Connecticut, Florida, Indiana, Massachusetts, Montana, New Hampshire, and New Jersey—have laws requiring sellers to disclose environmental problems with their property (such as toxic waste, radon, asbestos, or oil-tank leaks).

Many real estate boards now encourage sellers to fill out dis-closure forms, both to reduce agents' liability and to help protect the seller. Agents who do not tell buyers about a known defect in a property can be held liable later on, but the onus to reveal a defect is increasingly being put on sellers.

When and What to Disclose

As an owner, you must either fix the defects or be prepared to reveal them to your agent and prospective buyers *before* you get an offer. Buyers today are not hesitant to sue sellers and real estate agents over unknown property defects they later discover, so it pays to be honest. Sellers must disclose latent defects that aren't readily detected during a walk-through of the property, or risk being sued for misrepresentation.

Selling your house yourself does not relieve you from disclosing defects. Neither does ignorance, real or feigned. You can't, for example, claim that you didn't know the electrical wiring was faulty and then consider yourself absolved of responsibility if the house burns down after new buyers move in.

Disclosing defects, though it is onerous, can work in your favor. Prospects will value your honesty and feel they can trust you. Assuming your property is in good repair, a disclosure form also allows buyers to compare your property favorably to others. If your property has defects that you either can't or don't want to fix, such as high radon levels or the existence of a nearby stream that occasionally floods your property, reveal them now rather than find yourself involved in a lawsuit later.

Other problems that must be disclosed include easements and encroachments on the property; damage from foundation settling, or from flooding, fire, earthquakes, or other disasters; and any common areas or driveways that are shared with surrounding homes.

It may seem unfair to have to mention problems over which you have no control, but the alternative could be worse. If the buyers sue, you might have to take back the property and pay damages as well. Of course, don't go to excess. You don't have to remind buyers about the peeling paint or a crack in the window; these problems should be apparent during a walk-through of the property.

What You Must Tell the Buyer

Some of the most common items you should disclose to a prospective buyer involve those problems that are not immediately visible, or perhaps may not show up for some time after the buyer is living in the house. They include the following:

☐ structural defects, such as serious flaws in the foundation, walls, plumbing, electrical system, or septic tank

- ☐ chronic flooding of the basement during heavy rains or spring thaw
- ☐ additions or repairs that are not up to code or were made without the correct permits
- ☐ environmental hazards, such as radon, asbestos, lead-based paint, or contaminated soil
- ☐ neighborhood noise problems, including a nearby airport, fire station, or train tracks
- ☐ any lawsuits against you that may affect the property
- ☐ zoning violations, nonconforming uses of the property, or any violations of local subdivision setback requirements
- ☐ any negative or notorious associations connected with your property (see the "Haunted Houses" box following)

Condos or Co-ops. If you are selling a unit in a condominium or a cooperative building, you must make the following disclosures to interested buyers:

- ☐ any litigation pending against the condo association or co-op corporation
- ☐ any assessments you are aware of that are planned for the near future by the co-op corporation

HAUNTED HOUSES AND OTHER "STIGMATIZED" PROPERTIES

Do you have to tell your buyer that the house is "haunted" or was the scene of an especially lurid murder or suicide? Disclosure regarding these so-called stigmatized properties is a thorny issue. To date, there have been few court cases dealing with these situations. In 1983, an appeals court in California heard a case of a home in which a multiple murder had occurred a decade before the sale. The court agreed with the buyers that the murders could be a material factor affecting the home's value (neither the seller nor the real estate agent had informed the buyers of the crime).

In a 1990 case in New York State, a supreme court judge ruled that the seller did not have an obligation to reveal to buyers her belief that ghosts inhabited her property, since the state subscribes to the doctrine of *caveat emptor*, or "let the buyer beware." In most states this doctrine no longer holds, so this ruling cannot be broadly applied.

Most state laws require that anything that materially affects a property's value on the market must be disclosed to buyers. Though it's clear that structural defects lower a home's value, it's much less evident that psychologically disturbing events do the same. Because this area lacks sufficient legal precedents, there is no definitive answer at this time. But if a well-known murder or suicide took place in your home or on your property, you should probably disclose that fact to any prospects seriously interested in the home.

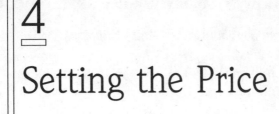

4

Setting the Price

The first step in putting your home on the market is to determine the true market value of your property. This figure may well decide whether you sell now, later, or perhaps not at all.

Until the end of the 1980s, most homeowners expected that their homes would automatically increase in value over the years. Today they have learned there is no guarantee that the worth of their real estate will appreciate or even keep up with inflation.

There are other considerations as well. As a proud homeowner, you may tend to overestimate the value of your property. Pride, fond memories, and unfounded expectations may lead you to ask an unrealistic price for your home. Certainly you would like to recover, at the very least, what you paid for it originally plus the money put into it for improvements. Unfortunately, the market doesn't always cooperate with even our most reasonable desires, and sellers who cling to a preconceived, unrealistic asking price will have a difficult time attracting agents and buyers to the property.

If the slow market perks up, however, eager home sellers may have their homes priced well below the demand. That's another reason why it's essential to know what similar houses are selling for in your market area.

Don't be influenced by the price your neighbors got for their home six months or a year ago. You need to know what houses in your neighborhood are selling for *right now*.

THE APPRAISAL

To find out your home's true market value—that is, the highest price your property can command in a competitive market—you should get appraisals from a number of experts in the field. First, ask several recommended real estate agents or brokers in your area to give you a *comparative market analysis*, or CMA.

The Comparative Market Analysis

To do an accurate analysis, agents visit your home and take notes on its location, size, condition, architecture, age, and various features. They then use computers to gather descriptions and sales prices of *comparables*, those homes in the area that resemble yours and have recently been listed or sold. The more closely a property matches your own, the less guesswork is involved in coming up with your home's market value. Descriptions provided by agents include photographs of each comparable home, specifics about items included in the price (carpets, appliances, custom window treatments), the length of time the home has been on the market, and whether any price reductions have taken place.

How accurate are CMAs? Most agents prefer to price homes as close to market value as possible. In a soft market, they may even choose to underprice your home slightly in order to make it appeal to more buyers, and thus sell faster. It's wise to ask several agents to do a market analysis. You can double-check the figure each one projects and make your own judgment on the final price for your home.

As a rule, you should take the *average* value, assuming the

GAUGING THE LOCAL MARKET

Many factors in your area can influence your home's market value, among which are these:

Employment.   What is the state of the economy in your part of the country? Check with the Bureau of Labor Statistics or the *Statistical Yearbook*, published annually by the National Data Bank of the U.S. Department of Commerce and available at your local library. Ask your local planning board or economic development office for your area's employment growth rate.

How Many Houses Are on the Market?   If there are a lot of new and older homes for sale, you might have to set your price lower.

How Quickly Are Homes Moving, Once They Come on the Market?   A real estate agent can give you this information. If most homes are on the market longer than three or four months, your price will need to be adjusted accordingly.

What Are Similar Houses Selling For in Your Area?   Compare their location, features, and condition to that of your home. Again, a real estate agent can provide this information.

Are Mortgage Interest Rates High or Low?   Falling interest rates may give a boost to home prices, since lower rates often encourage people to buy. If interest rates are rising, home prices will reflect the tougher mortgage environment and the harder time buyers have in qualifying for loans.

Carefully read the classified advertisements in your local newspapers to find out the asking prices for houses in your town or neighborhood that are similar to yours. Remember, though, that *asking* prices are not *selling* prices.

numbers from each agent are in the same general range (within about 5 percent). If you're in no rush to sell, list at the higher price; if you're anxious to sell, list your home at the lower end of the scale. *If one agent's price is substantially higher or lower than the others, find out why.* He or she may have over- or underrated some attribute of your property, or given more weight to a negative aspect, or even overlooked a particular feature.

Of course, agents may legitimately disagree. One agent may think that the asbestos-insulated pipes in your basement reduce your home's value, while two other agents may feel it's a negligible factor. You must decide which belief is valid, or get a fourth opinion. Or you can allow buyers and their home inspectors and/or lenders to determine the seriousness of the problem and whether it substantially affects the price. The truth will probably depend on several factors: the condition of the asbestos and whether or not it can be encapsulated; lenders' views on providing mortgage loans to buyers of houses containing asbestos; your state's laws regarding removal and disposal of asbestos; and how common asbestos-covered heating pipes are in your region of the country.

Keep in mind that some features of your home, such as a swimming pool, a three-car garage, 15-foot ceilings, or several modern art sculptures on the front lawn, may not be seen as assets in the eyes of real estate agents, appraisers, or buyers.

Occasionally an agent may inflate the value of your home in order to persuade you to list the property with him or her. This happens more often with expensive homes because potential buyers for these residences are assumed to have more money and may not be as careful—or as interested—in getting a lower price. A sale of this size also means a big commission for the agent. But, on the whole, an experienced agent will have a good idea of what your home is worth in today's market.

Of course, you make the final decision on price. If you insist on a higher price than is recommended, however, the agent may refuse you as a client or wait to show the property until you adjust your price to a more realistic level. What usually happens, though, is that no buyer is found, you get discouraged by low bids or no bids at all, and you reduce the price or take the home off the market.

Hiring a Professional Appraiser

Another option, especially if you are selling your home yourself, is to hire an appraiser to determine your home's market value. Professional appraisals can also give you a better idea of your home's marketability in a difficult or sluggish market.

The difference between a CMA submitted by a real estate agent and a professional appraisal is that appraisers have been trained to use available market data (such as comparable recent house sales), calculations of replacement cost, physical depreciation of systems and elements, economic obsolescence (a decline in your home's desirability owing to an increase in traffic through your neighborhood or a change in zoning that results in commercial construction of a gas station, office building, store, etc.), and logical analysis to arrive at a market value. Appraisers will also check out the interior of the home and its size, layout, and condition. They have no physical access to comparable homes, however, as does the real estate broker or agent.

What Appraisers Look For. The most important factor in any estimate is the *location* of the home. Is it in a well-kept residential neighborhood with other owner-occupied homes? Is it across the street from a store, gas station, or other commercial building? If it's a condominium or co-op, how well maintained are the building and grounds? The more residential, safe, and attractive the neighborhood, the higher the property value.

Another rule of thumb is that property located an accessible distance from a metropolitan area, where many people work, is generally more valuable than property in a more remote area.

The property's external *condition* also influences the appraisal figure. If your home needs exterior repainting or other cosmetic repairs, make them before the appraiser or real estate agent pays a visit. If extensive fix-up work is required, you'll have to decide whether it's worth the time, energy, or money. Your decision should be based on local market conditions and how quickly you must sell.

Another important factor is *age*. Homes that are 1 to 7 years old command somewhat higher prices than older homes, which tend to have more maintenance problems, older appliances, electrical or plumbing systems that may not be up to standard, and asbestos. Well-maintained homes over 60 years old, however, can bring higher prices, because buyers may perceive them as charming and well constructed.

Appraisers consider whether *zoning* and *property size* allow your home to be converted to some other use, such as a multifamily home or an office building.

Appraisers may be more objective than agents or brokers because they are not trying to acquire your listing.

In a volatile, rapidly changing market, low or conservative appraisals are common. If an appraisal comes in lower than you expected, you can challenge the figure through an appraisal review board. (The appraiser will not do another appraisal.) You must provide data supporting your contention that the property is worth more—based on your own research or from data supplied by a real estate agent. If the appraisal board concludes there is room for doubt, it will send another appraiser to conduct a second appraisal, at no charge to you.

Cost. A report from a professional appraiser runs about seven pages, and is specific and much more detailed than an analysis from a real estate agent. For their services, appraisers charge about $400; real estate agents do not charge for an analysis on your home's value. For this reason, it is debatable whether the cost is worth it for the typical residence, especially because the comparison method employed by brokers and agents is fairly accurate most of the time. A professional appraisal may be worthwhile, however, for an unusual home or expensive property with which there are few or no other comparable properties on the market.

Bank Appraisals. Once you have accepted an offer for your home and the buyer has been approved for a mortgage, an appraiser hired by the lender will come to check out your home and property. Because lenders base the amount of the mortgage loan on the appraised value or purchase price, whichever is lower, a low appraised value can cause problems for a buyer seeking to assume a large mortgage. Your listing agent can do you a service in this situation: he or she can accompany the bank appraiser on the inspection and answer any questions that affect and support the agreed-on price of the home.

TAX ASSESSMENTS

There are other ways to estimate your home's market value. For example, you can check your community's registry of deeds for prices and addresses of homes that were recently sold. Deeds don't provide a description of the homes, however, so all you can do is drive by the properties to see if they look similar to yours. Or simply check out comparable homes in your neighborhood that have recently been sold. If you know their selling prices as well as their condition, features, and number of rooms, compare their tax assessments with yours. If you don't know what the homes sold for, ask a real estate agent or check town or county property tax records at your county clerk's office.

If your home's tax assessment is higher than that of comparable homes, you may be able to price your home higher. The key word is *may*, because assessments are often based on variables. For example, a corner property is often taxed higher than other properties on the street, although it is not more desirable to buyers. The same can apply to houses with wide or large lots in areas where small lots are more common.

If no homes have sold recently in your neighborhood, tax assessments can only give you an idea of the *relative* value of your home, not its current market value. Bear in mind also that a tax assessment is frequently only a percentage of market value—such as 50 percent—substantially less than actual selling prices. The *Multiple Listing Service* books used by real estate brokers can tell

FINDING AN APPRAISER

In 1989, Congress passed a law requiring credentials for real estate appraisers who work for a lender that carries federal insurance. In most states, however, there are no legal standards for appraisers. To protect yourself, hire an appraiser who is a member of a professional appraisal organization that conforms to the Uniform Standards of Professional Appraisal Practice, which ensures that an appraiser meets certain ethical guidelines.

Appraisal organizations include the following:

American Society of Appraisers, P.O. Box 17265, Washington, DC 20041; 703-478-2228

Appraisal Institute, 875 North Michigan Avenue, Suite 2400, Chicago, IL 60611-1980; 312-335-4100

National Association of Independent Fee Appraisers, 7501 Murdoch Street, St. Louis, MO 63119; 314-781-6688

National Society of Real Estate Appraisers, 2555 M Street, N.W., Suite 301, Washington, DC 20037; 202-785-4477

Some appraisers have initials after their names, to signify that they have higher qualifications, education, or experience. Not all such credentials are significant, but some, such as MAI (Member, Appraisal Institute) and SRA (Senior Residential Appraiser) designations, granted by the Appraisal Institute, or IFA (Independent Fee Appraiser) designation, from the National Association of Independent Fee Appraisers, do carry weight. An appraiser with the MAI designation handles both residential and commercial appraisals. An appraiser with the SRA designation handles only residential appraisals.

you the percentage of market value on which your town bases its tax assessment. If the assessment was done more than a few years ago, though, the figures are probably out of date.

Ask an agent to provide you with a computer printout of sales in your town. These lists are usually available through the Multiple Listing Service, and contain descriptions as well as addresses and selling prices.

Or attend "open house" showings of similar properties. Take a firsthand look at the condition of these homes, their features and drawbacks, and how they compare with yours in terms of price.

THE RIGHT PRICE

The key to selling your home in fewer than six months is to price it fairly at the outset. Interest is highest during the first month of a new listing, when brokers make a point of seeing new properties, and buyers perceive them as fresh on the market. If you set the price too high—even with the intention of reducing it later—buyers will probably pass over it and favor other, more reasonably priced properties. A price that's too high makes many buyers reluctant or embarrassed to make a low offer, out of fear it will be too far below your expectations, even though the bid might well be acceptable.

If your house stays on the market many months, brokers may lose interest in showing it. Current buyers may speculate that something is wrong with the property because it hasn't sold. If that happens, you may have to wait for a new group of buyers, or even take your home off the market for a time and then try to sell it later at a more reasonable price.

If you've already bought another home or have other pressing reasons to sell, setting a lower price on the property will help you sell it faster. There's a saying that every home has a buyer—if the price is right.

As a selling technique, you can use "supermarket" pricing and set your asking price below benchmark figures—for example, $199,000, not $200,000. Then, if three months go by without an offer, consider cutting the price by 5 or 10 percent. If you are desperate to sell, you can also offer buyer financing, such as taking back a mortgage for the buyer at a below-market rate (when rates are high), giving a mortgage to someone who doesn't quite qualify for a bank loan, or offering to pay the cost of a home inspection, closing costs, or points.

In general, the listing price for your house should be about 15 percent more than the appraised market value. In a slow market, set your asking price about 10 percent higher than market value. Buyers today are knowledgeable about the market and are looking for reasonably priced properties, if not outright bargains.

If it's a seller's market, you can set your listing price as high as 20 percent above the expected selling price. Then, if you don't get any bids, you can work the price downward, the theory being that when prices are rising because of demand, it's better to aim high than sell low.

Other exceptions to listing your house at 10 to 15 percent above market value are if you're in no hurry to move, or can't afford to move unless you get your full price. Perhaps you'd like to buy a new house in a more expensive area, or you bought at the peak of the market and stand to lose tens of thousands of dollars if you sell at current prices. In such cases you can always test the market by listing at the high end (20 percent above market value) and cutting the price later, if necessary.

Reducing the Price

If you don't get any offers after a couple of months or so, you can cut your home's price by $5,000 to $10,000 to show that you're willing to negotiate and attract a bigger pool of prospects. A reduced price may encourage former prospects to come back for a second look. Avoid repeated price reductions, though, since buyers may wonder if some defect has forced the discount.

The quicker you make a reduction, the faster you're likely to sell. Buyers' interest in your property will be higher than if you wait five or six months to lower the price. But don't start out overpricing your home with the *intention* of making reductions; you'll waste time, and a string of price cuts will give the appearance of desperation. If you are eager to sell, you'll then have to make reductions until you start getting offers.

Price Inclusions

It's not wise to include in the sales price furniture, artwork, sculptures, or other items that aren't a fundamental part of your house. These movable items can always be negotiated later with a potential buyer. If you add them on to the price, they clutter up the sale and make it difficult for buyers to know exactly what they would be paying for the house. Besides, many buyers are not interested in those extra items.

Major appliances such as ovens, dishwashers, and washer/dryers are generally included in the sales price. So are chandeliers and other light fixtures, unless you specify otherwise. Because buyers often assume that most built-ins come with the home, you must let them know immediately if you plan to remove them. To avoid confusion and altercations later, remove any special items that you don't want sold with the house *before* you put it up for sale. List all items to be included in the sales sheets, and add them to the contract.

If you do remove a light fixture, door knocker, switchplates, or other similar item, replace it with another. If a buyer walks through the home a couple of days before closing and finds you've unexpectedly removed a chandelier from the dining room, he or she may be able to break the contract or at least ask for compensation.

Attached fixtures, such as a range and a built-in dishwasher, are considered part of the property. You must replace them with similar appliances if you plan to take them with you. (It's wise to install brand-name appliances because buyers recognize and desire them.) Refrigerators, washers, and dryers are not fixtures, but you must specify in the contract whether you plan to include them in the sale, sell them separately, or take them with you.

Wall-to-wall carpets are almost always included in the price;

area rugs, curtains, and drapes usually are not. If you have draperies, blinds, or shutters that were custom-made to fit unusual windows or doors, you probably should include them in the purchase price. It is *not* a good idea to tack their cost onto your asking price, however, since they may not be to a buyer's taste, their "used" value won't be the same as when they were new, and the buyer may plan to remove or change the existing items.

5

Getting Your Home Ready for Sale

In heated markets, buyers typically look at only five to ten houses before making an offer. In an attempt to secure a home before someone else—and before prices escalate—they are more willing to invest the time and money to fix certain problems. In addition, they are confident that they'll get back what they invest in the house when they eventually sell.

In sluggish markets, on the other hand, buyers are more cautious and spend more time looking for their "ideal" home. Indeed, they may look at 30 or more homes before even making an offer. The worse the market and the choosier the buyer, the more important it is to have your home in good condition. A number of relatively inexpensive steps can greatly improve your home's appearance and increase its market value.

FIRST IMPRESSIONS

Buyers can be either intrigued or discouraged by their first glimpse of your home. *Curb appeal* is a term used by real estate agents to assess the attractiveness of your house as seen initially from the street. Prospective buyers who don't like their first impression may not want to see the inside of the house, especially if they've been shopping around for some time.

Take an objective look at your home. Try to remember when you first saw it. What did *you* like about it? Has it deteriorated since then? Have its major flaws been fixed or improved? Have you kept the house attractive and current in terms of exterior maintenance and landscaping?

Walk down the street in both directions past your house. Is the siding free of blisters, cracks, and warps? Are the bushes and shrubs trimmed and healthy-looking? Are there pretty flowers or plants to soften and enhance the line of the building? Walk up to your front door. Is the walkway in good shape? What kind of image does the front door project—cheap, poorly maintained, and indifferent, or welcoming and attractive? How do the driveway, garage, and side yards look? Is the area cluttered with old porch furniture and toys, or is it lush and inviting, with a good lawn and shady areas?

Compare your house with other houses in the neighborhood. There may be something particularly attractive about a neighbor's house that you can imitate, such as adding a brass mailbox and house numbers, installing window boxes or planters near the front door, or replacing your plain concrete walkway with a brick or stone path. What do you do if your neighbors' lawns or walkways on either side of your house are in need of seeding or improvement? Depending on your relationship with them, perhaps you can offer to help.

If a neighbor's house looks especially shabby and neglected, and you're afraid it will hurt your chances of selling your own home, you have several choices. You can speak to the neighbor privately; draw up a petition signed by neighbors requesting that the house be fixed or painted—pointing out that a neglected property brings down everyone's property values; or contact your town hall's construction official to complain. Most towns have property maintenance codes or ordinances that require homeowners to keep their properties to a certain standard. Homeowners in violation of those codes are given notice to correct the problem and can be fined if they don't comply within a certain period of time.

In the case of condo and co-op owners, neighbors can appeal to the condo association or co-op board regarding similar problems—e.g., odor or excess noise from another unit, an illegal washing machine hookup that causes flooding, or a lack of carpeting in an upstairs unit. Condo or co-op owners who are unhappy with the exterior maintenance of the building can sue their association or board to comply with bylaws regarding building maintenance.

Exterior Problems and Improvements

Your house should look attractively individual, but avoid the overly personal or the unusual. If the mailbox, doormats, and front door all proclaim "The Wilsons," the Andersons may have a hard time picturing themselves in the house. Similarly, if the exterior colors are unconventionally bright, you will have a harder time selling. Many buyers do not have the imagination to envision a pink house painted white. So unless you're selling in an up market, it's best to appeal to popular tastes and stick to neutral off-whites, grays, and beiges. Shutters or trim can add some needed contrast to the overall look of the house, but keep to clean, outdoor colors, such as darker greens, blues, or reds.

Here are some other buyer turnoffs:

- cracked, blistering exterior paint or broken or dirty siding
- a fence, deck, or garage door in need of paint or repairs
- an ill-fitting, dirty, or scratched and chipped front door
- ripped screen doors
- dirty windows
- weeds and untrimmed shrubs and lawn
- cracked or crumbling walkways and steps
- a driveway in need of repaving
- broken glass in windows or doors

- ☐ light fixtures that are broken, rusted out, or missing bulbs
- ☐ a broken or rusted mailbox
- ☐ loose handrails
- ☐ missing house numbers
- ☐ a roof with curling or missing shingles

All of these signs of neglect may frighten away buyers who wonder what else hasn't been done to maintain the home over the years. Even superficial problems can lead them to expect high fix-up costs later on. But, except for a leaking roof that needs to be repaired or replaced, almost all of these defects can be fixed fairly inexpensively. And you can make many of the improvements yourself.

BASIC EXTERIOR IMPROVEMENTS

Here are some steps you can take to make your home more attractive:

- ☐ A good paint job in a neutral color pays back as much or more than its cost, even if you hire a professional to do it.
- ☐ If the paint on your house is merely dirty, or if you have vinyl or aluminum siding, wash it down.
- ☐ Plant flowers or place pots of annuals near the front door or walkways and in areas of the backyard that are in clear view of someone touring your home.
- ☐ Use bark chips to mulch in and around flower beds or between shrubs that show bare spots.
- ☐ Invest in landscaping to dress up or rejuvenate a barren or overgrown yard. It may be worth the cost to reseed or resod a scraggly lawn.
- ☐ In warmer months, take advantage of a terrace or patio

> by grouping freshly painted patio furniture attractively around a barbecue.
>
> ☐ Add a seasonal decoration to your door or steps, such as a garland of spring flowers, Indian corn at Thanksgiving, or pumpkins at Halloween. Refrain from using excessive holiday decorations or religious statuary or emblems.
>
> ☐ Clean up. Don't overlook a simple cleaning-up as a way to improve your home's curb appeal.
>
> Also make sure:
>
> ☐ the walkways and grounds are free of snow, leaves, and debris
>
> ☐ outside toys are picked up and stored away from walkways and stairs
>
> ☐ lawn furniture is clean, rust-free, and attractive
>
> ☐ garbage cans have lids and are stowed in an unobtrusive spot
>
> ☐ the front and back doormats are clean and in good condition
>
> ☐ the garage door is kept closed
>
> ☐ the number of cars in the driveway and street in front of your house is kept to a minimum
>
> Avoid keeping trucks and other commercial vehicles near your home. Do not park cars on any lawn areas; visitors may get the impression there is not enough driveway or garage space.

Interior Problems and Improvements

A number of conditions inside your home can also negatively influence buyers. Again, there are inexpensive, easy steps you can take to remedy these situations.

Eliminate Odors.   One basic problem for most buyers is odors, especially pet odors. Your nose may be accustomed to Fido's smell, but visitors will notice right away. They'll also notice Fluffy's used litter box. And many people are allergic to pet hair and dander. If you have a dog or cat, keep its eating and sleeping areas and litter boxes clean and odor-free. If possible, keep the food dishes and litter boxes out of sight, or at least remove them when prospective buyers are coming by. In warm weather, ventilate pet areas and place some lightly scented potpourri nearby. Shampoo carpets periodically.

Some cooking odors can be offensive. However, the aroma of baking bread, cakes, and cookies is enticing and appealing. Baked apples in the oven or boiled apples on top of the stove are some other favorite aromas.

If you smoke, keep your home well ventilated, ashtrays clean, and cigarettes preferably out of sight.

Emphasize Lightness and Brightness.   All of us respond positively to light, bright rooms. Not only are such areas cheerier and more inviting, but they make the house appear larger and more open. Even if your home isn't equipped with cathedral ceilings, skylights, patio and French doors, doors with sidelights and fanlights, recessed lights, bay windows, greenhouse windows, and other expansive uses of glass, you can make the most of the light it does admit by keeping windows and doors clean and free of dust and dirt. Use minimal window treatments, and pull aside curtains or blinds during the day. Don't block windows with tall furniture or shelves full of knickknacks.

Other ways to emphasize light:

- Brighten up dark corners and hallways with lamps and high-wattage bulbs.
- Use light colors on walls and ceilings.
- Hang strategically placed mirrors in small rooms.
- Light-colored furniture makes rooms look brighter. If you

need to reupholster or re-cover furniture, use light, cheerful colors or patterns.

□ Keep rooms neat and uncluttered.

□ Cut back any outside shrubbery or trees, especially on the north side. They may cast too much shade and block the sunlight. Some large trees on the south side of the house are advantageous, because they provide shade and cut down on cooling costs in the summer.

Clean and Paint.　What goes for the outside applies also to the inside. Keep the interior clean and neat, and paint wherever necessary. Obviously, if the layout and size of the home do not meet some buyers' needs, an attempt to present a sparkling and bright residence is unlikely to make them interested. But even if everything about the home is perfect, they may well be driven away by a dirty, cluttered house.

Above all, keep your home clear of stacks of magazines or newspapers, dirty ashtrays, and too many knickknacks. Keep toys confined to a toy box or some other closed container. Empty wastebaskets and garbage cans, and keep recyclable materials out of sight. Keep the family room clear of most personal items (a few family photos are fine), so that buyers can imagine their own objects in the room.

If you don't want to do a thorough, top-to-bottom cleaning yourself, hire a cleaning service. In fact, you might consider using a cleaning service weekly or biweekly during the selling period. If you can't face the task of clearing out years of accumulated, beloved clutter, hire someone to do it for you.

Pay particular attention to the following areas:

Walls and Ceilings.　Are they dirty, with fingerprints, paw prints, or other smudges? Wash them down with a good detergent or spray cleaner. Do walls or ceilings have cracks or peeling paint? Are they painted or wallpapered in bright, unusual, or large patterns? Are they covered with dark paneling? If so, it's time to repaint in light, neutral shades. Make sure there are no telltale signs of former leaks on the ceiling.

Dark paneling can be painted over, or wallpapered with an embossed wall covering designed to hide flawed walls. The paper can then be painted with latex paint. Painting rooms white or cream will make then look larger and brighter, too. Vacuum out any cobwebs, paying particular attention to corners and ceilings.

Wallpaper that is peeling can be glued down with adhesives designed for that purpose and available in hardware stores. Of course, torn and badly marked-up wallpaper should be replaced.

Flooring. Have your carpets professionally cleaned. If they have numerous stains or are worn, remove or replace them. In the kitchen and bathrooms, replace scratched or damaged vinyl floors. Don't waste money on top-of-the-line products; buyers frequently change the flooring anyway.

Wood Floors. If they are badly scuffed, scratched, or stained, have them sanded and varnished. Or you may be able to buff and polish them yourself, using rented equipment. Many buyers value good wood floors. A couple of coats of polyurethane have the added advantage of reflecting light back into a room to make it look brighter.

Windows and Curtains. Replace torn or worn curtains; launder dirty ones. Tie back curtains and keep shades up and shutters and blinds open during the day.

Clothes Closets, Linen Closets, Broom Closets, Laundry Rooms, and Under-Sink Areas. Are they tidy, or are clothes and other items piled on the floor? Not only do buyers feel uncomfortable seeing this mess, but they may suspect there isn't enough storage space. You can make storage spaces look bigger by clearing them out and removing out-of-season items. Throw out anything you don't need. Buy baskets for extra storage space, or install a closet organizing system.

Making Necessary Interior Repairs

Home buyers are on the lookout for every deficiency in a home, from a wet basement and signs of termites to malfunctioning or old heating and plumbing systems and inadequate wiring. The cost of repairs may actually be low, but home inspectors say some buyers overestimate the cost of fixing defects by 150 to 200 percent. Failing to repair even minor problems, such as loose doorknobs, dripping faucets, cracks in walls or ceilings, or windows that don't close properly, can kill a sale.

Again, look at your house with an objective eye. Maybe you're used to living with a bathtub that doesn't drain properly, a toilet that runs continuously, or electrical service that doesn't provide enough power to run an air conditioner and a vacuum cleaner at the same time. But buyers may not want to put up with those inconveniences. They might not detect these problems initially, but sooner or later their real estate agent or a house inspector will discover the defects.

Here are items to check and put in good working order before the first prospective buyer walks through your home:

Lights and Outlets.   Replace burned-out bulbs, clean light fixtures, and repair or replace cracked fixtures or nonfunctioning outlets. Many buyers check for adequate outlets, so make sure you have one for every 12 feet of wall. Outlets within 5 feet of a water source should have ground-fault circuit interrupters.

Faucets.   Eliminate drips and uneven or spurting water flow. Uneven flow may be caused by a dirty aerator, which can be cleaned or inexpensively replaced; a "stop and go" flow is caused by a loose cartridge and washer. If water seeps around edges of faucets or spout when turned on, the problem is probably either worn packing inside the faucet or a bad O-ring on the stem of the faucet, both of which can be fixed by a plumber.

Toilets.   Fix running, poorly flushing, or "rocking" toilets. Rocking indicates that the seal between the toilet and the floor has worn away; to prevent serious water damage to the ceiling below, it must be fixed immediately. Replace handles that stick, take more than one try to flush, or are broken.

Sink and Bathtub Drains.   Fix clogged or slow-flowing drains and repair drains or levers that don't close properly. Have all drains checked and cleaned out.

Water Pressure.   When you flush the toilet, does a running shower change temperature or become weaker? If your water pressure is poor, consult with a plumber about how to correct it. The solution could be as simple as replacing a dirty aerator or as involved as replacing pipes inside the home or outside, from the front of the house to the curb.

Plumbing Fixtures and Pipes.   Repair dripping pipes, cracked or old fixtures, and eliminate banging and rattling pipes. Rattling may be caused by a loose strap that is not holding a pipe to a ceiling or wall as it should. Banging may also be caused by a loose strap or severe water pressure, which can be corrected by installing a new air hammer or reducing valve.

Doorknobs.   Tighten or replace ill-fitting doorknobs, and polish tarnished ones.

Doors.   Make sure they can be opened and shut without sticking or scraping. Clean off finger marks around doorknobs. Pay particular attention to the front door: Check that house numbers, door knocker, kick plate, and metal sweeps at bottom are secure. Fix or replace a door that is crooked, warped, or loose. Paint if necessary.

Windows and Screens.   Repair cracked panes, broken or ripped screens, and windows that stick or don't open.

Heating and Air-conditioning Systems.   Check gas or oil furnaces for pressure and efficiency. If your heating bills seem higher than they should be, the furnace may need cleaning, repairing, or replacing. If you have a hot-water boiler, check the pressure after it's been running awhile. If the pressure exceeds 20 pounds or is less than 10 pounds, the boiler needs repairs. If you have a central air-conditioning system, make sure it is working properly and cools quickly and quietly to a comfortable level. If you have room air conditioners, make sure they are in good working order.

Electrical System. To ensure there are no problems with your electrical service or hookups, ask your electrician to inspect it. Most buyers want at least 100 amps of power. Buyers also prefer circuit breakers over fuses, because of the higher number of amps they more easily provide, and the ease of throwing a breaker switch compared with replacing a fuse.

Appliances. These should all be in working order. Clean the oven and defrost the refrigerator.

Sump Pump. You should install a sump pump if you have flooding or puddles in your basement after it rains. If you have problems with an existing pump, it may need replacing. (It is not effective to repair a sump pump because of the labor costs involved.) If your basement is used as living or working space, consider installing a sump pump as a safety measure against an overflowing washing machine, leaking boiler, etc.

Termites or Carpenter Ants, Rodents, High Radon Levels, Loose or Crumbling Asbestos, a Wet Basement. Correct these problems *now*. A serious buyer will uncover these through a home inspection, termite inspection, or radon test, some or all of which may be required by your state or the buyer's bank or mortgage company. If so, you may lose the sale or have to reduce your price substantially to accommodate the buyer.

RADON

Radon is an odorless, colorless, naturally occurring radioactive gas formed by the decay of uranium in the earth's crust. Exposure to high levels in the air in homes poses a significant risk of lung cancer. Radon enters homes through the soil beneath or adjacent to a home's foundations and through cracks, drains, utility entry sites, and other openings in basement walls and floors. Radon affects homes in all 50 states, and many buyers want a home tested for radon before going ahead with a purchase. You can test your home for radon levels inexpensively and easily in a matter of days with charcoal canisters, or over several months with alpha-track devices. The latter are more appropriate for measuring long-term average levels. Many hardware stores now carry both types of radon detectors.

If your house has an elevated radon level, the problem can be corrected fairly easily, in most cases. Common solutions, depending on the level of radon and the climate in your area, include increasing natural ventilation, especially in the basement or source area of the radon; sealing off cracks, crawl spaces, and joints in walls and floor; and/or installing a forced-air ventilation system.

For more information, contact your state's public health department or department of environmental protection.

ROOM-BY-ROOM IMPROVEMENTS

Take a leisurely walk through each room of your home, noting areas to be upgraded or improved. Put yourself in the place of the buyer: What would attract you and what would draw your attention in a negative way? Sometimes the change can be just a vase of flowers or a new quilt to perk up a bedroom. Other additions or repairs can be more elaborate, such as new wallpaper, fresh curtains, a new rug, or new cabinets.

Kitchens and Bathrooms

These are the rooms that can make the difference in whether or not someone decides to buy your house. Cramped, dark, ill-equipped, or old-fashioned bathrooms and kitchens lower the value of your home considerably. Remodeling a kitchen is expensive, so a house with an up-to-date, attractive kitchen has a big advantage over a house without one.

All appliances and fixtures must be in good working order. Keep rooms and their fixtures and appliances spotless; even the interiors of appliances and cabinets should get a good cleaning, since buyers often look inside them.

The brighter and lighter you can make the kitchen and bath, the better. Again, think in terms of light paint, window coverings that can be pushed aside or pulled up to let in more light, high-wattage incandescent light bulbs (fluorescent bulbs cast a bluer, cooler light that is less appealing), and sparkling clean windows.

If your kitchen cabinets look old or shabby, consider refacing or repainting them. Painted cabinets or a refrigerator that is scratched and chipped can be refinished.

Here are some other tips for improving the kitchen area:

☐ Clean out drawers, cabinets, shelves, broom closets.
☐ Keep counters clear of appliances, dishes, food, and other items.
☐ If cabinet hardware looks old-fashioned, upgrade handles and pulls.
☐ Add warmth and visual appeal with green plants or a vase of flowers.
☐ Keep countertops clean; eliminate stains and mildew in sinks and grouting with bleach, vinegar, and water, or a commercial product.

Make your bathrooms more attractive by doing the following:

☐ Regrout or recaulk the tub if necessary. Keep caulking around the tub in good condition, because water can get into the wall and cause leaks in downstairs walls.

☐ Re-enamel a cast-iron bathtub that is rusted or stained. Look under "Bathroom Remodeling" in the Yellow Pages for porcelain reglazing or resurfacing specialists.

☐ Replace broken ceramic tiles on floors or walls.

☐ Replace a moldy shower curtain with a plain white one; white looks clean, adds light, and makes small rooms look larger. If you prefer a fabric curtain over a plastic liner, choose a subdued or lightly flowered pattern.

☐ Invest in a new bath mat and matching towels. Or put in new wall-to-wall carpeting made especially for bathrooms; it gives the room a luxurious look and feel.

☐ Clean out drawers, cabinets, linen closets, and medicine chests. Reorganize items to reassure buyers that there is adequate storage space.

☐ Upgrade towel racks and faucet fixtures, if necessary. Brass fixtures add an elegant touch.

☐ Store all personal hygiene items out of sight.

☐ Place a basket of potpourri or scented soaps in each bathroom.

Living Room

The living room should look inviting and comfortable, but not too casual. Clear shelves and tables of most small items to make the room appear more spacious, and don't let family photos take up too much space. Avoid the bare-walls look, however; paintings or inexpensive prints warm up a room and add interest.

If the room looks crowded, move some furniture into storage. Rearrange the furniture around a focal point, such as a fireplace or sofa and coffee table. Adjusting the placement of furniture can also improve traffic flow. Well-filled bookshelves, either built-in or standing, add color and interest to a room, as do a few green plants.

If upholstery is dirty and worn, have it cleaned, cover it with throws or pillows, or invest in new slipcovers. If you think prospective buyers might wish to sit, make sure there are tables nearby on which to place drinks and paperwork.

While subdued and neutral colors work best for walls, ceilings, and carpeting, add warmth and character by using colorful pillows, scatter rugs, prints, plants, candles, and other accessories. Easily changed and portable objects are an inexpensive, quick way to update the color scheme and make your home more memorable and appealing.

Dining Room

The dining room should present a more formal appearance than other rooms in the home. Ideally, you want prospective buyers to be able to picture themselves enjoying a family gathering or an elegant dinner in the room. So don't let your dining room table become a dumping ground for papers, mail, and other odds and ends.

Keep the table polished, with an attractive centerpiece of fruit or flowers. Make sure the chandelier is dust-free and all the bulbs are working, and keep the chairs pushed under the table. A pair of candles adds a romantic touch. An area rug placed under the table and extending a few feet outward on all sides helps "anchor" the space and make it look warmer.

If your dining room is boxy and lacking in architectural features, consider adding some inexpensive ceiling and chair-rail moldings to dress it up. Buyers are drawn to detail work that adds interest and a feeling of craftsmanship and luxury to otherwise plain rooms.

Family Room

Even though the family room is meant to be the most casual room in the house, it should still be neat and clean. Don't leave magazines, glasses, shoes, toys, or other personal items lying around.

If you have a fireplace, place a couple of armchairs or couches on either side to create a cozy conversation center, and draw attention to it with an attractive, simple mantel display or a large painting above the mantel. Again, keep surfaces relatively clear, although a dish of candy, a fancy bowl, a vase of flowers, or a handsome coffee-table book adds an inviting touch.

Children's Bedrooms

Hard as it may be on your children, remove most of the movie posters and pictures of rock stars, keep toys stowed away, and hang up clothes neatly. The key is to depersonalize and remove 95 percent of what others might see as "junk." To prevent a mutiny, have your children select a few items to keep on display.

Master Bedroom

The master bedroom is a place to relax and retreat from the outside world, as well as a place to sleep. The softer, more inviting and romantic you can make this room, the better.

Wall-to-wall carpeting is preferred by most buyers here and in the other bedrooms, too. The colors should be muted and the bedcovers luxuriant, with coordinating comforter, dust ruffle, pillow cases and shams, and curtains or shades.

A writing desk, loveseat, or chaise longue makes a desirable private sitting area. Keep closets orderly, and remove all off-season clothing to a basement, attic wardrobe, or under-the-bed storage boxes. *Always* make sure the bed is made up before showing the house, or before agents show it.

Problem Areas: Attic, Basement, and Garage

These areas are frequently cramped, dark, and just plain ugly. We tend to pile our old junk and discarded items here.

Eliminate mess and clean up dirt, cobwebs, and—on the garage floor—oil stains (use sawdust or cat litter to soak up the oil).

Other suggestions:

- Paint the concrete floor and walls in your basement white to make the rooms look larger and brighter.
- If you have a water problem in the basement, fix it! Installing a sump pump is the most common solution. French drains, which leave a one-to-two-inch gap between floor and walls, are another, although they can aggravate an existing radon problem. Waterproofing basement walls, regrading soil to slope away from the foundation, and redirecting gutters, leaders, and downspouts to empty farther away from the foundation also help.
- If your basement is damp, ventilate it by opening the windows. Buy a dehumidifier if you plan to sell during hot, humid weather.
- Buy inexpensive shelving, pegboard, wall hooks, and plastic or wire baskets for tool storage. Clean out your garage so the buyer can envision fitting his or her car inside with room to spare.
- Place a few sachets or air fresheners strategically in musty-smelling areas.
- Use high-wattage bulbs to add lighting in dark corners.
- Call the exterminator if you have problems with mice, squirrels, bats, or insects. Eliminate any signs of their former existence—such as traps, dishes of poison, droppings, sawdust, piles of termite wings, or holes in the roof, eaves, or walls.

ENHANCE THE POSITIVE, DOWNPLAY THE NEGATIVE

One of the keys to making your house attractive to prospective buyers is to emphasize its positive aspects and modify or gloss over its less attractive ones. Does your house have a big yard? If so, highlight this feature. Keep the yard mowed and cleared of excess furniture, garden tools, and toys so that buyers can see its true size and potential for enjoyment.

DEPERSONALIZE YOUR HOME

If your personality or opinions come through too strongly in furnishings or interior design, buyers may feel uncomfortable or be offended. Too many personal items may make them feel like intruders and prevent them from imagining themselves in the house.

- ☐ Try to eliminate strong personality statements, such as wall murals, loud wallpaper, or unusual colors of paint. Redecorate or paint in neutral colors, if necessary.
- ☐ If you have a lot of monogrammed items—such as a mailbox, doormats, kitchen plaques, towels, and awards or sports trophies—remove or replace some of them in favor of less personal objects.
- ☐ Keep knickknacks and collectibles to a minimum. You may love and value your collection of matchbook covers, antique cuckoo clocks, or Elvis memorabilia, but to someone else it may just be clutter.
- ☐ If you own unusual pets, such as a monkey, piranha fish, rats, or snakes, give them to a relative or an aquarium during the selling period.
- ☐ If representations of a particular animal or object are rampant throughout your home, whittle down the collection so you don't discourage a buyer who doesn't share your enthusiasm.
- ☐ Remove any expressions of your religious, political, or sexual views. Get rid of anything that might offend someone else or that voices a strong opinion, such as a gun cabinet, *Playboy* calendars or pinup magazines, teen-idol posters, or antismoking signs.

Do you have a working fireplace? Clean and paint the mantel, and remove debris and ashes from the fireplace. Attractive fireplace equipment can draw the buyer's eye to it. In cold months, stack logs in the fireplace. In warm months, a large vase of flowers or a basket of dried flowers in front of a fireplace is a nice touch.

Negative aspects can be downplayed as well. Make a small yard look larger by grouping bushes in different locations to add eye interest and break up the sightlines. Similarly, make small rooms look larger by painting them off-white or a light color, keeping furniture to a minimum, drawing attention to windows and the view beyond by using valances or other nonobscuring window treatments, and by hanging mirrors and framed pictures to distract the eye. The old decorating trick of using vertical-striped wallpaper in a low-ceilinged room increases the sense of height. And architecturally plain rooms can be dressed up inexpensively with ceiling and baseboard moldings.

Be careful how you decorate to alter a negative feature. If a window looks out on an unattractive view, you can hang a large plant or insert a lacy panel to obscure it. But if you try to hide the view completely with a heavy curtain or a pulled-down shade, buyers will be tempted to see what's behind it. Well-kept plants are a nice touch for warming up a sterile-looking room. Don't carry the greenhouse theme too far, though, because overdoing plants, like overdoing any decorating scheme, overwhelms the room and detracts from its positive features.

A PRE-LISTING INSPECTION

A pre-listing inspection of your home, which you arrange and pay for, can uncover defects that could discourage buyers or work against you during negotiations. An inspection typically costs between $250 and $500 and takes about two to three hours. The cost will vary depending on the size of your house and what part of the country you live in.

Today, more than 90 percent of home buyers in major met-

YOUR NEIGHBORHOOD

Are there advantages to living in your neighborhood that you think buyers and real estate agents should know about? Here are some possibilities:

- ☐ You have particularly helpful neighbors.
- ☐ A convenient bus or train route is nearby.
- ☐ You are within walking distance of schools or parks.
- ☐ Your street has little traffic, making it relatively safe for children and pets.
- ☐ Your street is congenial and community-minded. There's a block party every year, and neighbors get together for softball games in the summer and an open house at Christmas.
- ☐ There are many children in the neighborhood, thus providing friends for a child.

Keep in mind, however, that what seem advantages to you may not be to others. Buyers who value their privacy may not be delighted by block parties or softball games.

Use your discretion. If you are selling your home yourself, listen to what buyers reveal about their likes and dislikes. Don't simply announce facts that certain prospects might view as negatives. If they ask whether you have friendly neighbors or children in the neighborhood, you can tell them about the big Fourth of July barbecue and the large number of children on the street. If you are using a broker, make a list that you or your broker can use on the fact sheet for your house.

ropolitan areas request a home inspection before they sign a contract. Obviously, the seller who recognizes that his or her home will probably be inspected by the buyer, and that disclosing problems now can prevent more serious ones later, can gain a competitive edge by having the house inspected for flaws beforehand.

Home inspection experts report that nearly half of resale homes have at least one major defect. Sellers who commission a pre-listing inspection, and either correct the problems or disclose them to agents or buyers, help prevent a potential lawsuit later.

If your home is in excellent condition, the inspection report is better than your word and helps to justify your asking price. Get the results in writing, to protect yourself in case there are problems after the sale.

A typical home inspection examines visible structure as well as plumbing, electrical, and heating and cooling systems, the roof and visible insulation, walls, ceilings, floors, windows, doors, foundation, basement, septic tanks, and wells.

Texas is at present the only state that licenses home inspectors. In other states, people can call themselves a home inspector, whether or not they are qualified. One way to ensure a professional home inspection is to hire a member of the American Society of Home Inspectors. ASHI inspectors must meet professional, educational, and experience criteria and conform to the organization's code of ethics. For a free brochure about home inspections and a list of ASHI members in your area, send a self-addressed, stamped business-size envelope to ASHI, 1735 North Lynn Street, Suite 950, Arlington, VA 22209-2022. ASHI members and other home inspectors are also listed under "Building Inspection Service" in the Yellow Pages.

An alternative to hiring a home inspector is to hire individual tradespeople you know or for whom you have recommendations — a plumber, electrician, and carpenter. They have a better mastery of their respective fields than do most home inspectors. For a fee, they will provide you with an oral or written report on the condition of your home's mechanical systems and structure. They will also suggest what improvements should be made.

If you are concerned about environmental problems such as radon, asbestos, and termites, contact your state's department of environmental protection or the U.S. Environmental Protection Agency for a list of approved inspectors in those fields.

Before the inspector arrives, make sure he or she has easy access to all areas, including the attic, basement, crawl spaces, and storage areas. Accompany the inspector on the tour of your home so you can ask questions and get problems clarified. Some inspection services will ask you to fill out a disclosure form detailing what you know about your home's condition. Even if they don't, be prepared to answer as well as to ask questions, and to provide information on any current or potential problems your property may have. You'll get a more thorough inspection report and a better idea of what needs to be done to give your home a competitive edge in the market.

ASK REAL ESTATE AGENTS

If you find it difficult to look at your home objectively, or you want specific advice geared to your property, real estate agents can be a valuable source of information.

In return for listing your property with them, agents will make suggestions on sprucing up your home. If they don't volunteer such information, ask. They may be afraid of offending you, or your house may be in such good shape they see little need for improvement.

Some agents are willing to offer suggestions when they give you a comparative market analysis. They can then answer specific questions about the wisdom of particular improvements or the impact of certain features on price and marketability.

6

Selling on Your Own

Owners always have the option of selling their homes without the aid of a real estate professional. In the trade, a house for sale by its owner, or a person selling his or her own house, is called a *FSBO* (pronounced "fizzbo"), from "for sale by owner." About 20 percent of sellers choose to go this route.

The reward can be a saving of thousands of dollars on an agent's commission, which is typically set at 6 percent of the sale price. This means you could save $12,000 by selling a $200,000 home yourself. Some of that money will go toward advertising and marketing your home, of course.

There are other costs, many less measurable, if you decide to sell on your own. If you work long hours and have an inflexible schedule, you may not have enough free time to show the place and handle phone calls. Even if you do have the time, you must be willing to put up with the headaches that come with a personal sale, which we describe later in this chapter.

Some owners who bought at the height of the market and face selling at the bottom see cutting out the agent's commission as the easiest way to lower the price on their homes and not take so much of a loss. (Ironically, while a slow market may motivate owners to sell on their own, the best time to be a FSBO is in a hot market.)

But not all homeowners who go the do-it-yourself route are motivated strictly by the savings. Some are in no rush to sell, and want to see how they fare on their own; others have had poor experiences with agents or brokers and feel they can do better themselves.

SHOULD YOU SELL YOUR HOME YOURSELF?

The monetary advantages of selling on your own are obvious, but so are the disadvantages. You need time, energy, and motivation to sell your home successfully. You must set the price, advertise and market the home, hold showings and open houses, screen phone callers, evaluate how serious prospects are and whether they can afford your home, handle price negotiations, and possibly even direct buyers to mortgage brokers and other sources of financing. You must also be prepared to answer questions about your neighborhood and its schools and other community resources.

Other drawbacks faced by FSBOs are lack of access to buyers relocating from other states, which real estate agents get through company relocation programs; and the probability of not being included in the *Multiple Listing Service* (MLS). The MLS is a constantly updated inventory of all homes for sale in an area. It is a valuable, one-stop shopping tool for buyers and agents that allows them to choose the homes they want to see the most. Usually only brokers (who pay a yearly fee) can use it; some discount brokers may have access to it, but will charge their customers a fee for the service.

It's important to realize from the beginning that selling your home is a business transaction that puts you on the opposite side of the fence from the buyer. You'll be pushing for a higher price; the buyers will be pulling for a lower one. You will be negotiating for an as-is sale; they may want you to make repairs or improvements. You may not want to include certain appliances or other items in the sale that they insist on. Negotiating with buyers requires both firmness and flexibility. More than that, it means you must appear less emotionally involved with the home, and calm and in control at all times.

ALTERNATIVE MARKETING GROUPS

A slow housing market and the growing use of computers has resulted in an upsurge of entrepreneurial real estate groups that can assist sellers. Unlike the traditional real estate agent, they function as consultants in all areas of home selling, and charge a flat fee for their services.

Discount Brokers

Discount real estate brokers help you with paperwork, negotiations, following up on buyers' mortgage applications, and other tasks related to selling your home. They usually charge a flat fee or a commission of 1 to 3 percent of the selling price. For a higher fee, a few discount brokers will show your home to prospects.

Some of these companies will list your home in the Multiple Listing Service in your area for either a fee of a few hundred dollars or, typically, an additional 1 percent of the selling price. But expect to pay more—usually a total of 3 or 4 percent—if the discount broker finds you a buyer through the MLS. The extra money goes to the agent who brings the buyer to the discount broker.

One company that helps FSBOs market their homes is Buy Owner, a nationwide service based in Fort Lauderdale, Florida (800-771-7777). It offers the services of "home sale consultants"— licensed real estate brokers—for either 1 percent or 4 percent of the sales cost. Again, you pay the higher amount only if you choose to have your house listed in the MLS and eventually find a buyer through it. The company also offers a listing in a computer "match-making" system for about $400.

Other national chains also offer assistance with appraisals, mar-

QUESTIONS TO ASK YOURSELF BEFORE SELLING ON YOUR OWN

At first glance, selling a home by yourself seems fairly easy: you fix up the house, advertise it in the local newspapers, and wait for callers. As with any large purchase, however, buyers take their time about committing themselves, ask numerous questions, and are demanding and easily discouraged.

Before you put your home on the market, ask yourself these questions:

- ☐ Do you like dealing with people? Are you able to accommodate other people's schedules? Are you prepared to receive phone calls at any time of the day or night?
- ☐ Are you willing to show your home without notice when somebody rings your bell after seeing your sign?
- ☐ Are you nervous about letting strangers into your home?
- ☐ Do you have a preconceived notion about who should be living in your home, or are you flexible and openminded?
- ☐ Can you courteously and professionally attend to a parade of strangers who may—or may not—be interested in your house?
- ☐ Are you prepared to answer numerous questions about your property and community? Are you willing to do a little research about your town?
- ☐ Can you be enthusiastic—yet honest—about your property? If you are moving because you dislike your house, neighbors, or town, your negative feelings may well come through to prospects.
- ☐ How quickly do you need to sell? FSBOs usually take longer to sell, especially in a down market.

keting, writing and placing ads, negotiating a deal, financing, reviewing contracts, and showing your home. These are Help-U-Sell (800-609-4357) and WHY USA (800-733-7283). Their fees range from around $1,000 for a flat-fee service at WHY USA to 2.5 to 3 percent of the selling price at Help-U-Sell. The national average fee for both services is about $3,000, but can go up to $5,000 for homes selling for more than $175,000.

As with a standard broker, you pay the fee only if your home sells. The fees go up for listing and selling through the MLS. In fact, at WHY USA, sellers who aren't able to find a buyer through the flat-fee service, and agree to an MLS listing, pay standard brokers' fees of 5 or 6 percent if a broker brings them a buyer.

You may have better luck and pay lower fees by negotiating with local discount brokers, if any are in your area. Pick and choose from a variety of individual services offered by these brokers, including a For Sale sign, a lockbox, a listing with the MLS, or consulting advice at hourly rates. You can get as much or as little help as you want and can afford. To locate such a service, check your local newspapers or Yellow Pages.

Home Sellers' Networks

Another option is a home sellers' network. These entrepreneurs offer low-cost help in selling your home, primarily by charging a flat fee to put your listing into a computer data base, directory, magazine, or major newspaper. The listing may be available only to computer owners through a computer bulletin board, or it may be mailed out in printed form to buyers who call a toll-free number in response to the company's ads or to a For Sale sign in your front yard. More information on these services may be found in local newspapers, in the Yellow Pages, or through real estate magazines distributed in supermarkets and other outlets.

MARKETING TECHNIQUES

If you choose to sell a home on your own, you should first draw up a complete marketing plan. The plan should take into consideration several avenues for reaching buyers, including point-of-purchase signs, newspaper and magazine ads, circulars, fact sheets, an open house, and word of mouth. But first you have to determine who your buyers are.

Prospective Buyers

Who is your potential buyer most likely to be? A large family? A career couple? Empty-nesters? Singles? Newlyweds? The answer depends on the size of your house (especially the number of bedrooms) and yard, the condition of the house, its features, and its location.

Size. If your house has at least three bedrooms, a family room, and a large yard, it will probably attract families with children. If you live in a one- or two-bedroom condo, town house, or small single-family dwelling, you should market your home to singles or couples without children who don't need a lot of space and don't want maintenance headaches. Similarly, smaller yards usually appeal to people without children or to those who don't have the time or energy to maintain a larger property.

Some more extensive layouts, often found in so-called mother-daughter homes, appeal to large or extended families or families who need home office space.

Condition. A house in top condition attracts people who don't have much free time or energy to fix up a place, typically career couples, families, or older couples. Houses that need work may appeal to younger buyers, especially first-time buyers on limited budgets, investors, or one-income couples with a spouse at home who is able to do fix-up work or oversee hired workers.

Historic houses attract a small segment of the market, usually buyers who have the money and often the free time to put into major upkeep and renovation.

Features.   The more outstanding features your house has, the more expensive it will be. It will probably appeal to move-up buyers with children, established career couples, relocated buyers, or older couples who can afford a trade-up house. Features can include a large number of rooms, luxurious materials, state-of-the-art kitchens and bathrooms, and extras such as fireplaces, decks, skylights, Palladian windows, and decorative wood moldings.

Location.   If your house is located on a busy road, a family with small children or pets may not want to live there. If the size of your house still makes it appropriate for families, try installing a fence around the property (if you don't already have one). Obviously, a house on a cul-de-sac has a big advantage if families are your prime prospects.

Parks and nearby schools also attract families. Shopping areas, regular bus service, and train stations appeal to everyone, especially retired people, singles, and working couples.

If your neighborhood is full of children, chances are other families will want to live there also. The children will have playmates and the parents will have a built-in network of other parents to help them adjust to a new area. On the other hand, a quiet neighborhood with a majority of older couples will suit more-mature buyers.

Your home's location also influences the *type* of buyer you should try to attract. Is your town or section of town working class, middle class, upper middle class, or upper class? Knowing your neighborhood and its general ambience helps you define the income of your buyers and what types are likely to be interested in your home: singles or families living on a tight budget, professional couples, traditional one-income families, or wealthier buyers. Prospects usually look for homes that reflect their tastes and fit their own self-image or aspirations. Some people prefer a friendly, casual neighborhood; others value the privacy, peace, and lower cost of living of a rural community; still others desire the status of a prestigious area.

The same can be said for style. A cozy Cape Cod may suit a young couple, but it would lack the status an executive may seek. A Colonial or split-level may be perfect for a growing family, but would not appeal to a retired couple, who may prefer the one-level living offered by a ranch, or the low-maintenance living of a condo or co-op.

THE FAIR HOUSING LAW

The Civil Rights Act of 1866, the Federal Fair Housing Law (Title VII of the Civil Rights Act of 1968), and a subsequent amendment, declare that discrimination based on race, color, religion, sex, or national origin is illegal in the sale or rental of most housing. The aim of these laws is to prevent sellers or landlords from denying to a particular buyer that housing is available for sale or rent when it is, in fact, available. It also prohibits sellers or landlords from setting discriminatory conditions and limitations on who may buy or rent property. Real estate agents are also prohibited from steering buyers away from or toward particular neighborhoods because of race, religion, or skin color.

People selling their homes on their own, as well as brokers and agents, are not allowed to discriminate against buyers or renters on the basis of race, religion, color, national origin, ancestry, marital status, sex, or physical handicap.

The Importance of a Sign

Your first step is to put up a noticeable, plainly lettered For Sale sign in your front yard. If you live in a condo or co-op where outdoor signs are not allowed, put one in your most visible window.

A sign can be your most effective marketing tool—as it is for most real estate brokers—especially if you are in a desirable location. Many buyers pinpoint the town and area of town they want to live in, then drive around looking for For Sale signs and jotting down phone numbers. Perhaps a neighbor or someone who periodically drives by your house has admired it for years and would love to own it. Even someone who wasn't in the market for a home may see your sign and suddenly become interested.

The sign should be in keeping with the size of real estate brokers' signs in your area, so you don't exceed any size restrictions in your town. Some exclusive areas prohibit signs, so check on restrictions with your town's building department.

Make sure your phone number is prominent, as well as the words "For Sale" or "For Sale by Owner" on both sides. A white sign with black or red letters stands out best and is the easiest to read. Place the sign close to the street and perpendicular to it, so it is visible to traffic from both directions. If your home has special features, such as a fourth bedroom, fireplace, family room, two or more bathrooms, or large property, list one or two items on the sign, too. If you want to preserve your privacy and decrease the chance of unexpected visitors, put "By Appointment Only" on the sign.

You can purchase a sign from a sign company (look in the Yellow Pages) or sign painter, or you can make one yourself. Remember, it must look neat and professional. Stay away from the small Day-glo red-on-black paper signs sold by hardware stores. They are too small and look cheap. Besides, phone numbers written on these signs are difficult to read.

Newspapers and Circulars

Marketing your home may cost $50 to $200 or more, depending on where and how frequently you advertise, how aggressively you conduct your search for a buyer, and how quickly you find a likely prospect.

Advertise in the newspapers in your area that offer the most comprehensive real estate sections—that is, the most articles and classified ads. Compare circulation figures to help you determine the size of the market you are reaching. Stick to the area papers, because the market for sale-by-owner homes tends almost always to be local. Relocating or out-of-town buyers usually use the services of real estate agents.

It pays, though, to advertise in the Sunday classified real estate sections of major newspapers. Sunday is the day most buyers are able to examine the ads carefully, make phone calls, and visit open houses. The cost for a six-line ad in a major Sunday newspaper in the Northeast runs about $50; the weekday price is about half that. You may get a discount if you run your ad for several consecutive days.

Small-town newspapers are another good place to advertise — if they offer a real estate listing of at least one or two columns. You can measure the effectiveness of such advertising by the response you get after one or two tries.

Do you belong to a professional society, club, church or synagogue, civic group, parents' network, or some other organization that publishes a newsletter? If it carries ads, get yours included. If it doesn't, maybe no one has ever broached the issue; it certainly doesn't hurt to ask.

Scout out homes-for-sale publications in your area. Usually these circulars are found in supermarkets. Although most are published by real estate brokers or associations, some may be geared toward FSBOs. The price of a one-eighth-page ad with a small photo starts around $30.

If you can feature a picture of your house instead of just a descriptive listing, do so unless you feel a photo will discourage buyers. A photo might actually hurt sales in the case of a house that looks poorly maintained, one that looks much smaller than it actually is, one built in an unusual or hodgepodge style, or one that is invisible behind overgrown shrubs or trees (a problem you should correct anyway before putting your house on the market).

Assuming you've fixed visible defects and improved the curb appeal of your house, a good, clear photo catches buyers' attention much more readily than plain copy. Photos taken in the spring and summer look more attractive than winter shots, but your photo should be timely and geared to the selling season. If it's February and you show a picture of your house as it looked in the fall, buyers may wonder why it hasn't sold. When you take the photo, make sure there are no cars or people in front of the house or in the driveway. Some publications may offer the services of a professional photographer; check whether there is an additional fee.

How to Write an Effective Ad

How well you write your ad greatly affects response. The goal is to present your house in the best possible light without distorting the facts. You run the risk of alienating or even angering prospects if you exaggerate, prevaricate, or leave out critical information. If your house is next to a gas station or a busy highway, for example, buyers will understandably be upset if you write "quiet residential area" in the ad.

That doesn't mean, however, that you need to mention the gas station. Besides, if you have a fence, trees, or a tall hedge blocking out the view and much of the noise, the gas station may not be a problem to buyers who like your home. On the other hand, a nearby highway is a plus, so you can write "easy access to highway," "close to main roads," or "quick commute to city."

Proximity to shopping, downtown, schools, parks, or houses of worship will appeal to some buyers. Often, being within walking distance of such facilities is more desirable than being on the same block with them. You have to decide whether to mention such factors, based on their impact on your property, their attractiveness, and who your potential buyers are. Families with young children will probably appreciate proximity to a playground or school much more than will single people or empty-nesters.

Phrasing drawbacks in a positive way can alert buyers to their existence, thereby eliminating those who would truly not be interested in your neighborhood, and also help buyers see potential problems in a better light.

When selling a house next door to a high school, write "close to schools." Stating "next door to high school" would discourage buyers. When prospects call or visit, you can explain that the school next door has an attractive front lawn, that the neighborhood is otherwise quiet, and that your yard is private because of the trees that screen your house from the school and road.

If your home is small, it's best to write "perfect [or "ideal"] starter or retirement home." *Starter home* usually means a lower-priced or two- or three-bedroom residence. That eliminates prospects who want a move-up home, but it also focuses in on the segment of buyers likely to be most interested in your residence.

Your ad should run about five to seven lines long, unless you have a luxury property or one with many different features (such as "Restored Victorian, 6 bedrooms, 3 baths, original pressed-tin ceilings, front and rear staircases, pantry, slate roof, 3 fireplaces, 2 acres, stocked pond, stream with bridge, barn, greenhouse, guest cottage").

Words Are Important. Using abbreviations saves money in an ad. Don't use too many, though, because house-hunters may get frustrated trying to decipher them. Use only abbreviations that are well known, such as "bdrm" for bedroom, "fpl" for fireplace, "CAC" for central air-conditioning, or "w/d" for washer/dryer. If in doubt, spell out the word.

Put the phrase "For Sale by Owner" in your ad. Generally it's seen as a benefit to buyers, who expect that you will pass on to them some of your savings on the commission. In fact, some buyers limit their search to FSBO ads. But you should realize that you will get phone calls from real estate agents seeking your business; a FSBO announcement serves as an open invitation to agents.

Unless your house is in bad condition or sits on an unusually large, attractive lot, don't stress property features, such as "professionally landscaped property" as a headline, because that may make buyers wonder about the condition or size of the house. Don't list every attribute, either; your goal is to pique buyers' interest and entice them to visit. A full laundry list of features might make

WORDS THAT SELL HOUSES

HEADLINES THAT STRESS VALUE

- First Time on Market
- Just Listed
- Price Reduced
- Owner Wants Offers Now
- For Sale by Original Owner
- Steal This Beauty
- Best Bargain in Town
- Must Sacrifice
- Owner Transferred
- Low Taxes
- Owner Financing
- Low Maintenance
- Move-In or "Mint" Condition
- Immaculate
- Well Maintained
- Below Market Price

Avoid words such as *desperate, anxious,* or *must sell immediately.* These encourage buyers to make low offers and put you at a disadvantage during negotiations. They may also scare off buyers who want house-hunting to be a pleasant, relaxed experience.

HEADLINES THAT STRESS LOCATION

- Fantastic View
- Country Estate/Country Charm
- Your Own Pond! (or brook, etc.)
- Cul-de-sac Location
- Quiet Street
- Low-Traffic Street
- Parklike Setting
- Secluded Setting
- Near Everything
- A Private Retreat
- Great Neighbors
- Quiet Residential Area
- Most Desirable Location in Town (or name the area, such as "West Side" or "Shadyside Boulevard area")
- Prime Location
- Executive Area
- Exclusive Section
- Sought-After Neighborhood
- Near (name of better town)

If your house sits near the border of a more desirable town, mention it. If buyers would love the status of living in town A but can't find anything they can afford there, living close by in town B is often the next best choice.

HEADLINES THAT STRESS FEATURES

In addition to listing any special features of your home, such as "central air," "beamed ceiling in living room," "large deck," or "wooded, private backyard," you can use more general phrases that stress overall features, such as these:

- Custom Built
- Perfect for Large Family
- Every Amenity

- Too Many Features to List
- Dream House (Dream Kitchen, Fantastic Master Suite, etc.)

HEADLINES THAT STRESS CONDITION

- Mint Condition
- Move-In Condition
- A Real Creampuff
- A Real Beauty
- Totally Renovated

- New Everything!
- Loved by Owner
- Executive Home
- Gorgeous Home
- Spotless Throughout

buyers prejudge your home and cross it off their lists. It's better to fill in the details later and handle objections in person.

Be specific about your home's attributes. Instead of just saying "cheery, bright home," say "skylights and French doors in kitchen" or "large bay window in living room."

Emotional Appeal. Use words that appeal to buyers' emotions, especially their desire for status, privacy, comfort, romance, security, peace, and beauty. Or appeal to their pocketbooks. In other words, stress the features of your home that have emotional appeal, as well as any advantage your home has—or that you can offer— that helps buyers save money.

Features that have emotional appeal include bay windows, cathedral ceilings, skylights, fireplaces, master bedroom suites, Jacuzzis, big bathrooms, walk-in closets, decks, patios, balconies, porches, attractive landscaping, a cul-de-sac or exclusive location, or a private setting.

Special features you can mention in your ad include the following:

- any new structural elements (roof, windows), rooms, or remodeled baths and kitchens
- a recently painted interior or exterior
- central air-conditioning
- entrance foyer
- eat-in kitchen
- breakfast area
- hardwood floors
- bay windows or Palladian windows
- fireplace or woodstove
- beamed ceilings
- built-ins, including bookshelves and cabinets
- patios, decks, and porches
- sun room
- greenhouse
- cedar closet
- main-floor or second-floor laundry area
- finished basement
- fenced-in yard
- professional landscaping

Whether you should mention vinyl or aluminum siding depends on how it is perceived in your area. In the Northeast, many buyers favor vinyl siding for its low-maintenance qualities. But in the Northwest, a lot of buyers prefer cedar or redwood siding.

If your house has many features, you don't have to mention them all. Instead, state "too many features to list" or "many other amenities."

You can take some creative license with your home's attributes as long as you don't mislead buyers. The owner of a small house should use phrases such as "charming," "storybook home," "perfect for newlyweds," "starter house in neighborhood of more expensive homes," even "low maintenance." Avoid the words *cozy* or *doll house*, which almost everybody instantly translates to "small."

If you have a Cape Cod that has a finished upstairs or family-room addition, write "expanded Cape Cod." If your house has room for easy expansion, either by converting an upstairs room or walk-up attic, or by adding a room over a garage, mention that fact.

Don't focus on features that are of interest to very few buyers, such as a darkroom, rec room ("finished basement" appeals to more buyers), sauna, hobbyist garage, or workshop. You can list them briefly at the end of your ad and in other promotional materials, but mention the other, more widely desired features first. A house with too many unusual or unique-to-owner features can make buyers feel it's the wrong property for them, before they even see it. In general, rooms built to indulge specific owner interests do not make a house easier to sell.

More-popular intrinsic features, such as a tennis court, a separate cottage, an attached office suite, or a basement that's been legally converted to a rental unit, can be mentioned up front to reach buyers who value these amenities. There may be fewer of these buyers, but they will pay more for a home with those features.

Where to Start. List your home's location (town) first, followed by the style of the house and information about the lot, street, or neighborhood. Then list the number of bedrooms and baths, extra or particularly large rooms, and special features. For example, if you recently enlarged your master bedroom, say "large master bedroom with separate sitting area" or "15-by-20-foot master bedroom." Instead of stating "big backyard," say "private backyard, 175 feet deep."

Example: "New Milford—creampuff Colonial on quiet street. Fireplace in living room, 3 bedrooms, 2½ baths. Master bedroom suite, his-and-hers closets, large eat-in kitchen with skylight, walk-in pantry, sun room, new deck, 60-by-175-foot lot. $180,000."

Above all, include your asking price. If there is no price listed, prospects will think that your house is too expensive and pass it by. At the least, they are likely to be annoyed by the omission, since price is a critical factor.

As a rule, avoid using the phrase "asking price," because it conveys the message that you are not confident about your home's value and may have set too high a price for it. Some buyers may also see it as an opportunity to make a low offer. In a soft market, it's better to lower your price gradually than imply that you are too flexible at the beginning. (Buyers in a slow market presume sellers are flexible anyway.)

Keep up-to-date with what's popular with buyers so you know the features to stress in your promotional materials. Read real estate and decorating sections of your local newspapers, be alert to renovations and additions made by local homeowners, and check the for-sale ads to see what features are repeatedly stressed.

To keep your ad fresh, write up several versions that you can rotate every couple of weeks. Buyers become tired of homes they see advertised week after week. Change your copy to fit the emotional appeal of the season, as well. In summer, use a headline such as "Entertain on spacious deck," "Cool off in your own pool," or "Central air." If winter is approaching, use "Cozy fireplace" or "Large living room, perfect for holiday entertaining."

In a buyer's market, you often need some attention-getting ploy for people to notice your ad and respond to it. Yours could be larger than the ones around it, with darker type or some kind of border or design. Or you could have the ad inserted in the main editorial part of the paper, where it will be noticed immediately. Buyer incentives such as "Free cruise to Bermuda included in sale" can also generate interest.

Prepare a Fact Sheet

A fact sheet describing relevant information about your house, neighborhood, and town is an excellent marketing tool. These fliers answer buyers' questions, can be retained by the prospect for future reference, and may lead buyers to think favorably of your property. They also give prospective buyers confidence that they are dealing with responsible, serious sellers. A fact sheet can also reinforce interest in your home and help create a sense of familiarity and attachment to it. Give it to people who tour your home and come to your open houses.

A flier is typically printed on 8½-by-11-inch, good-quality paper that is professionally typeset by a printer. It should display either a clearly reproduced black-and-white photo or a laser-copied color photo of your house, centered near the top. A color photo is more expensive, but makes more of an impression. One hundred fliers with a color photo typically cost $150.

You can also draw a floor plan of the home to put under the photo, on back of the flier, or on a separate attached sheet. A floor plan helps buyers recall your home's layout and dimensions. A contractor or architect may charge a couple of hundred dollars to draw a floor plan for you, depending on the hourly rate in your area.

The fact sheet should list all the important features of your home, from its style and location to the number of bedrooms and baths, including special appliances, lot size, recent additions or improvements, and price. If you are listing at a high price to test the market, however, or think you may have to drop the price in a month or two, omit printing the price. Type it in instead. This is preferable to having to cross off the price and give buyers the impression your house is not salable or was overpriced to begin with.

What to Include. The space limitations of a newspaper ad dictate that you list only the highlights of your house and property, but a fact sheet is the place to describe every positive feature. It should include a full listing of all the rooms of your home, and should point out any special features (such as a bay window in the kitchen, a double vanity, ceramic tile floors, or wall-to-wall carpeting). Other features that should be mentioned include:

- detached or attached garage (and size)
- dishwasher
- garbage disposal
- built-in microwave oven
- electric garage-door opener
- security system
- slate roof
- full basement, finished or otherwise
- recreation room
- main-floor laundry room

The fact sheet should also specify:

- type of heating system
- town water or well
- septic system or sewer
- lot size
- real estate taxes
- maintenance fees (for a condo or co-op)
- proximity to public transportation
- nearby houses of worship
- proximity of recreation facilities, parks, and playgrounds

Put your name, address, and phone number on the fact sheet—either near the photo at the top or at the bottom. Also include a small map and clear directions to your home. This will help buyers find your house again if they want to take another look.

Hold an Open House

Open houses are not a particularly effective way of getting qualified buyers to your home. Too often they draw only window-shoppers who don't have the financial qualifications to buy property, or they attract only curiosity-seekers, or potential home sellers attempting to price their own homes. In fact, many real estate agents admit that the true value of open houses is in how agents use them to make contacts with buyers and other potential sellers.

That said, however, open houses can draw a large number of prospects to visit your home. They may include those who have seen your sign and admired your home, even though they are not in the market to buy, as well as people who feel uncomfortable or pressured dealing with owners on a one-to-one basis and feel more relaxed in a crowd.

Even if you do not get many serious lookers, it takes only one to become a buyer. Open houses can attract people who might not otherwise come to see your home. The more desirable your community, the better your chance of attracting a large number of prospects.

Wait to see how well you do with other advertising methods before holding an open house. If you have a lot of lookers from your ads, but no bids and no serious buyers, after a few months try lowering your price. If that doesn't pull in buyers, *then* hold an open house. You can hold one every two months or so, to give new home buyers a chance to visit.

How to Prepare for an Open House. Start by enlisting the help of neighbors, relatives, and friends. Encourage them to invite anyone they know who's in the market to buy. To give the impression of much buyer interest in your property, have your friends come and tour as if they were buyers. Also, ask a couple of your closest and most sociable friends or relatives if they would be willing to help you greet or direct visitors in case the open house gets too busy.

To attract visitors, add an "Open House This Sunday" banner to your sign—or put up a separate sign—a week in advance. Post "Open House" signs with arrows at both ends of your street and on nearby well-traveled routes. List the hours of the open house on all signs. To help people find your home, and to make the event look festive, tie a bunch of balloons to the sign in front of the house. Run an ad in your local newspaper a few days before the event. Include the date and day, as well as your address, directions to your home, and your phone number.

The best day to hold an open house is on a weekend, when more prospects can attend. The best time of year is spring and early summer, traditionally the best time for selling real estate. Avoid holding an open house on a holiday weekend or when many people are otherwise occupied, such as on Super Bowl Sunday. On the other hand, if a local event such as an art show, historic house tour, or town celebration brings people to your area, plan your open house to coincide with the event.

Stick to the hours favored by real estate agents, typically noon to 4:00 P.M. in winter and 1:00 to 5:00 P.M. in summer. Put your fact sheet on a table near the door and ask visitors to sign a guest book. Ask for their names, addresses, and phone numbers, which will give you a mailing list if you later lower your price, decide to offer financing, or make a major improvement to the house.

You can also use the list to make follow-up phone calls to visitors to ask what they thought of your home. Hard as it is to listen to criticism of your property, talking to visitors is a good way to discover the problems and drawbacks of a home. You can use that information either to fix the problem or to lower the price.

PREPARING TO SHOW YOUR HOME

Before you show your home, it's important to do the following:

- ☐ Scrub the bathrooms and wipe the fixtures clean of water marks. Put out clean towels, shower curtains, rugs, and bath mats. Make sure the shades are up, the toilet seats down. Empty the wastebaskets and put personal items out of sight.
- ☐ Clean the kitchen sink, counters, and floor. Remove

fingerprints, spills, and clutter from appliances and counters. Wash and put away all dishes. Take out the garbage.

☐ Put away clothes, toys, and newspapers and magazines.

☐ Air out the house. Place scented soaps, candles, or potpourri in the bathroom (don't overdo it, though). If you have the time and inclination, bake bread or cookies before visitors arrive, for the aroma.

☐ Keep children confined to one area of the house, or send them over to a friend's house.

☐ Remove pets and their dishes and beds from the premises, if possible. Some people are allergic to animals; others are afraid of them. In any case, pets are a distraction.

☐ If it's a dark day, or if it's evening, turn on all the lights. Keep shades and curtains open at all times.

☐ If you have a fireplace and the weather is cold, light a fire. Be sure the damper is open, and no smoke escapes into the room.

☐ Place a few vases filled with fresh flowers on the dining room and kitchen tables, on the mantel, even in the bathrooms. Again, don't overdo it.

☐ Keep the temperature comfortably warm in the winter, cool in the summer. A too-cold or too-hot house makes an unpleasant impression, and visitors will want to leave quickly.

☐ Look professional. A sloppy or overcasual appearance conveys the impression that you don't care enough about the buyers to look presentable, or that you are not serious about selling.

Spread the Word

Neighbors, friends, working colleagues, members of your church or synagogue, your hairdresser or barber, your doctor, plumber, or carpenter — virtually everyone you know — are good sources of leads. Draw up a list of friends and acquaintances, and let them know your home is on the market. Speak to them in person or call, or mail a brief note attached to your information sheet. To encourage your contacts, you can offer an incentive, such as a free trip, concert tickets, or even a cash reward.

If you are hesitant about telling everyone your asking price, give a ballpark figure such as "the low 200s." Price is too important to be kept a secret.

SAMPLE LETTER

Dear Neighbor:

Would you do us a favor? We've recently put our house at 110 Elm Drive on the market. If you know anyone who might be interested in a three-bedroom, 1½-bath Colonial on a third of an acre in the Latchstring section of Oradell, please tell them about our property or give us a call at [phone number] so we can contact them. A fact sheet with more details is attached. [If you prefer to give out fact sheets only to true prospects, say "Asking price is in the low $200s. Fact sheets available upon request."] Thank you.

Sincerely, Joan and Joe Seller

P.S. If you find a buyer for us, we'll give you a $100 gift certificate to [name of big department store in your area] or $100 toward a dinner for two at the restaurant of your choice.

PRESENTING YOUR HOME TO A BUYER

When someone calls in response to your ad, sign, or mailing, be enthusiastic about your property. Concentrate on your home's positive features, and don't volunteer negative ones.

Answer all questions, but do not go into detail. If you do, you risk giving the caller a reason not to see your property; there's bound to be something about your home that doesn't fit his or her wish list. Your goal is to encourage callers to make an appointment. If you receive many inquiries, but prospects don't make appointments, the problem may be a misleading ad or the way you are handling inquiries on the phone.

Don't bore prospects with a long list of details about your home, but answer questions honestly and ask buyers when they would like to visit. At this early stage, maintain a flexible or neutral stance about issues that really should be dealt with later on, such as owner financing, possession date, and items to be included with the sale. If prospects press you on how low a price you would be willing to accept, tell them you don't want to discuss price until they've seen your property. You can simply say you are flexible or there is room for negotiation.

Have your spouse or a friend check your telephone etiquette; what sounds businesslike to you may sound brusque or aggressive to buyers. In any case, thank callers for their interest.

If people ask, "Why are you selling your home yourself?" be prepared with an answer. If you say, "To save money," prospects may think that they can make a low offer because you are saving on the commission. An effective answer is, "Because I think I can do a better job selling my home than a real estate agent can."

Give clear directions to your home, preferably via the most attractive route. If you feel you're losing a caller's interest, offer to mail him or her the fact sheet on your home. People rarely refuse such an offer, and there's always a possibility the sheet could change their minds. Or they might pass it on to a friend who is interested in buying a home.

Ask for the caller's telephone number, in case you have to

change the appointment. You can also use it to verify that the person is really living at that particular location. To avoid losing any prospective buyers, have an answering machine to take calls when you are not at home, or when you don't have time to talk.

Be prepared to answer buyers' inquiries about why you are selling. An unsophisticated or inexperienced seller can give answers to this question that can be interpreted in a negative fashion by prospects. Your motivation for selling may seem perfectly logical to you, but saying "We've outgrown the home" may make buyers wonder if the home is big enough for their families; similarly, saying "We've bought a bigger house" can reflect badly on your present one and make buyers see it as an opportunity to negotiate your price downward, since they will assume you are eager to sell.

It can work the other way, too. You might not think twice about revealing that you're moving to a smaller, more manageable place, but buyers might infer that your current home is a maintenance headache and possibly too expensive to carry. And if the honest answer to the query is depressing, such as divorce, serious illness, or death, refrain from mentioning the fact, if possible. Psychologically, these reasons may cast a negative pall on the property that is hard for some buyers to shake off.

So what should you say? Avoid giving any reason that might be construed as detrimental to the house or neighborhood. If you're being transferred, have accepted a new job elsewhere, or simply want to live closer to family members, go ahead and say so. Or just answer that your needs have changed.

Dealing with Agents. After you advertise your home, many of the calls you receive will be from agents who want your listing. Some will be pushy, some will merely want to mail you their business card in case you decide to list, and a few may even offer tips or a brochure on how to sell on your own. Be polite but firm. You may be determined now to sell your home yourself, but a soft market, a too-high asking price, a job change that limits your free time and makes a fast move imperative, or just plain bad luck selling on your own may change your mind in a few months or a year.

SAFEGUARD YOURSELF AND
YOUR HOME

One of the risks of selling your home yourself is possible confrontations with strangers. Thieves and other criminals, alone or working in pairs, have been known to prey on sellers showing houses alone. The likelihood of anything happening is remote, but for your own security and peace of mind, take a few simple precautions:

- ☐ Screen callers by asking for a phone number where they can be reached. Confirm all appointments by calling back the day of or day before the scheduled visit.
- ☐ Don't show your home alone. If no spouse is available, ask a neighbor or friend to be with you in the house. If you feel uncomfortable about such an obvious arrangement, ask your friend or neighbor to drop by "unexpectedly" during the prospect's visit.
- ☐ If you must show your house alone, tell a neighbor. You can even ask him or her to check on you if you don't call back within a prearranged time limit of a half hour or so.
- ☐ Remove or lock away all valuables.
- ☐ Throw away old prescription medicines, and lock up the rest. Be suspicious of anyone who seems particularly interested in repeated looks at the bathroom and the contents of cabinets.

So save the names and numbers of any agents who sound knowledgeable, experienced, and personable.

Sometimes an agent has a buyer in mind for your house, or maybe buyers spot your house while driving by with the agent, and want to see it. If you allow the agent to show the house, obviously you can expect to pay the agency's commission for that particular buyer if he or she makes an acceptable offer. Or you can refuse to allow the agent to show it, in the hope that the buyers in question will see your ad and call, or come back on their own.

Agents may promise to produce a buyer if you'll just sign an exclusive listing contract with them. Once you sign the contract (or after a 24-hour cancellation clause is up, depending on the state), your house may be tied up for at least several months, during which time the agent may or may not actually get you a buyer. A better arrangement is to continue to try to sell the house on your own, and allow agents to show it as well. This is known as an *open listing* (see chapter 7).

QUALIFYING BUYERS

This is a necessary but often uncomfortable aspect of selling on your own. You won't have the agent to ask the sensitive financial questions and to pre-screen buyers before bringing them to your home. If you don't qualify prospects yourself, you can end up wasting time with people who can't afford to buy your home. Even worse, you may find out the serious prospect you thought was a bona fide buyer can't get a mortgage.

Whether a buyer will be able to afford your home depends on income, debts (liabilities), credit history, current interest rates, the lender's flexibility, the price you and the buyer agree on for your home, and how much cash the buyer has for the down payment.

To determine a buyer's ability to sustain a mortgage, lenders apply what are commonly called the 36- and 28-percent ratios to gross monthly income. This means they allow as much as 36 percent of the buyer's income to be spent on total debt. Debt includes expenses and loans in addition to the mortgage payments of principal, interest, taxes, and insurance (PITI, in real estate and lender's parlance). In calculating this 36-percent ceiling on debt, based on a buyer's gross monthly income, lenders factor in any debts payable for longer than ten months, such as car loans and student loans. When other debts are excluded, lenders allow only a maximum of 28 percent of a buyer's income to be spent on mortgage expenses.

The government makes exceptions to the 36- and 28-percent ratios through its Federal Housing Administration (FHA) and Veterans Affairs (VA) loan programs. The FHA uses ratios of 29 percent and 41 percent of gross income; the VA uses a ratio of 41 percent of effective net income. Occasionally the government creates new programs to help home buyers—often, but not always, first-timers. For example, Fannie Mae, the Federal National Mortgage Association, offers a Community Home Buyer's Program that allows buyers to spend as much as 33 percent of their gross monthly income on housing payments. Total debt payments can be as much as 38 percent of gross monthly income, but buyers' income cannot exceed 115 percent of the median income in their area of the country. Buyers are also required to take home-buyer education classes. For more information on this program, contact Fannie Mae's Public Information Office, 3900 Wisconsin Avenue, N.W., Washington, DC 20016 (phone 800-732-6643).

In addition, lenders usually require that at least half of the cash used for the down payment and closing costs come from the buyer's own income, savings, or sale of assets or investments. If the buyer is planning on receiving a gift from relatives to pay for more than half of the down payment, he or she could have a problem with mortgage financing.

Questions to Ask the Buyer

If you have an interested prospect—someone who has come to see the house several times, and has expressed a serious interest to you—it may be time to check his or her financial background and expectations. Start the screening process by asking about the buyer's financial situation, and if the buyer has been cleared for a mortgage. Use judgment if the prospect appears to be offended by these questions; in a soft market, you do not want to risk losing serious buyers. However, asking the following questions can help weed out poor prospects from viable ones:

Have You Been Preapproved for a Loan by a Lender? If so, what is the maximum mortgage amount for which you are qualified? What interest rate and term?

If the mortgage amount is based on a medium or high interest rate on a 15-year loan, the buyer could afford a higher-priced home by taking a 30-year, lower-interest loan; the longer-term loan carries lower monthly payments. Or the buyer might be able to afford even more house if he or she applied for an adjustable-rate mortgage (ARM), where the interest rate typically runs 2 percent less than the rate on a conventional 30-year loan.

If the buyer hasn't been preapproved by a lender, your questions may persuade him or her to do just that. There's no charge, and the lender typically gives an answer immediately. Especially in a seller's market, buyers who are prequalified have an edge. If the buyer is not familiar with the prequalification process, explain that it saves time and prevents future problems when applying for a mortgage, whatever home the buyer finally decides to purchase.

Do You Own a Home Now? Are You Planning to Sell It Before You Buy? If the answer is no, ask why not. Most move-up or relocating buyers need the cash from the sales of their present homes to put toward the down payment and closing costs of a new one. Moreover, few buyers can afford to carry two mortgages. If the buyer insists on making the purchase contingent on the sale of his or her current home, your selling your home to that buyer faces a major stumbling block.

How Much Equity Do You Expect to Get from the Sale of Your Current Home? If the answer is "None," or "I'm taking a loss," proceed to the next question.

Where Will Your Down-Payment Money Come From? Here are the usual answers: from the sale of a current home; from savings; from investments, such as stocks, bonds, or life insurance; from a gift. If a buyer is planning on getting a loan from relatives or friends, this bonus will add to the debt load and make the buyer less desirable to lenders. And if the mortgage loan pushes the buyer's debt load above the 36-percent cutoff figure, the prospect may not be able to get the necessary mortgage to buy your home.

Do You Know What Kind of Down Payment Is Needed to Buy the Property? For example, you could say, "A 10-percent down payment on this house at its listing price runs around x dollars. A 20-percent down payment requires about x dollars. Do you think you would be able to put down that amount?" If the prospect hesitates or says no, remind the potential buyer of the sources listed above; maybe he or she is counting only cash in the bank. A buyer may also be able to sell a car or boat or some other asset to raise the extra cash.

Are You Aware that the Monthly Mortgage Payments on Your House (at Its List Price with 20 Percent Down) Will Be in the Range of x to y Dollars at Current Interest Rates? The reaction to this question should give you a clue to how serious a buyer is about your home. At that point, a prospect may well eliminate your home from his or her list.

To figure out the monthly payments, purchase an amortization table at a bookstore. Look for a table that includes loan amounts up to at least the cost of your home minus a 10 percent down payment. Make sure the interest rates cover current rates available from lenders. (To find out current rates, check the real estate sections of the local newspapers.) The table gives instructions on how to figure out the monthly mortgage payment.

Have You Set Aside Money for Closing Costs? These costs—including points charged on conventional loans by lenders—are usually 6 to 8 percent of the *mortgage amount* (not sales price). *Example:* A house sells for $200,000. The buyers put down $40,000 and take a mortgage for $160,000. They can expect to pay about $9,500 to $12,500 in closing costs and loan fees (see chapter 9).

For ideas on helping a buyer cut closing costs or finance a down payment, see chapter 9.

The answers and reactions to these questions should give you an idea of a prospect's ability to afford your home. If buyers indicate they like what they see and your home is at the top of their price range, you can probably expect a low offer. Of course, buyers may *say* your home is a stretch for their budget as a ploy to get you to be flexible on price. But in that case, you'll enter negotiations prepared for a low offer.

Buyers' Needs

While you are showing your property, listen carefully to what buyers have to say. By asking questions tactfully and in a conversational manner, you can find out a great deal. Pay particular attention to their family's size, their reason for moving, how far your house is from their work, whether they have special needs, and their reactions to certain rooms.

If a buyer comments favorably on the Colonial-style trim in the dining room, for example, point out the antique (or reproduction) Colonial light fixture in the foyer. If a buyer likes the ceramic tile backsplash in your kitchen, mention that it is hand-painted by a local artist, that the tiles are an unusual, expensive type imported from Italy, and so forth.

Try to assess buyers' needs and preferences. Are they looking to move in six months, when school is out? If so, see if you can accommodate them. Ask what they're looking for in a house. If your home falls short in one or two areas, point out how easy it would be to convert a space to another use, add a deck or put on an addition, or change the layout.

By listening carefully and watching buyers' body language, you can learn a lot about what they react to, and whether your home comes close to meeting their needs. Even if they have minor objections to your home, by being flexible and creative, you may still be able to put together a deal.

SHOWING YOUR HOME

Your dress, demeanor, and actions can greatly influence people's feelings about your property. If you are pleasant, helpful, and calm, visitors are likely to feel comfortable in your home. If you are anxious, rushed, or overeager, visitors may feel ill at ease and simply want to leave. Think about how you would like to be treated if you were a prospective buyer touring somebody else's home, and treat your visitors the same way.

Avoid exhibiting the following behaviors:

- □ Breathing down prospects' necks. Give them enough space to wander freely through the rooms, but stay close enough to answer questions and point out special features they might miss.
- □ Seeming anxious or desperate to sell.
- □ Talking too much. It can be distracting and annoying to prospects who want to concentrate on observing your home and picturing themselves living there.
- □ Stating the obvious, such as, "This is the kitchen."
- □ Becoming defensive about your home's drawbacks. Admit that your yard is small or the appliances are old; buyers can see those things for themselves. And being straightforward about drawbacks will convince buyers that you will be realistic during negotiations.
- □ Hiding faults or making false statements about the age or condition of your house, the safety of your neighborhood, or the traffic on the street.
- □ Distracting buyers from the house by talking about your

furniture, possessions, recent vacation, children, and so forth.

□ Rushing buyers through your home. Let them set the pace.

□ Letting buyers' negative comments upset you. Some buyers use criticism as a negotiating tactic to prepare you to accept a low offer; others just "talk out" their reactions without thinking about your feelings. In fact, when prospects do a lot of talking and focus on the little problems, such as whether the closets will hold all their clothes or whether the breakfast area will seat everyone comfortably, that's often a sign that they are seriously considering your property. If a home isn't right for buyers, most often they won't say much or they will make a general statement such as, "The rooms are too small."

To get the most out of a showing:

□ Be warm and welcoming. Treat buyers as you would guests, but allow them the freedom to examine your home.

□ Speak enthusiastically and positively in describing your house, town, and community.

□ Point out those features that prospects might miss on an initial walk-through, such as the walk-in closet in the pantry, or the central vacuum system.

□ Guide buyers in an organized manner through your house, from first floor to second and up to the attic if they ask, and then down to the basement. If you have a choice between two rooms opposite each other, show the most impressive one first. Let your visitors enter each room first and look around a minute by themselves so they can focus on the room—not on you—and to increase the sense of spaciousness. Encourage them to walk into the middle of the room and to open closet and cabinet doors.

□ Allow buyers time to go back and look at rooms alone and discuss your home privately.

□ Offer information that buyers may have no way of knowing.

Tell them about any new structures or features, and mention appliances or floor coverings that will stay with the house. If the beams or moldings are original to the house, let buyers know. If the floor is oak or the front door is mahogany, reveal that information. If they're seeing your home in the winter, tell them about the patio and flower gardens that turn the backyard into a delightful place for entertaining in warmer months. Even better, show them photos.

☐ Provide printed information on anything relevant: new tax breaks or other legislation affecting home buyers; mortgage rates; homeowner's assistance or state or government programs that provide financial assistance; and community or neighborhood activities and programs.

☐ Prepare a folder of information pertinent to your property. Prospective buyers will ask questions about your home and property. The following ones can be expected, and you should be prepared to answer them:

☐ What do you pay in property taxes?

☐ How much does it cost to heat and cool your home?

☐ What do you pay for gas and electricity?

☐ What do you pay for water, and who supplies it?

☐ How old are various structural components and systems, including the roof, water heater, furnace, and plumbing system?

☐ How old are any appliances that will stay with the house?

☐ Do you have any guarantees or warranties on appliances or components of the home, such as siding or roofing, and are these warranties transferable?

☐ Are there any fees for municipal or private services, such as garbage pickup, and what are those services?

☐ Do you have town sewers, or are you on a septic system? (You should know when your septic tank was last cleaned out, and how often it needs to be cleaned.) Where is it located on the property?

- □ Do you have well water or town water? (If your water comes from a well, it should have been tested, and you should have a report on the results.)
- □ Is your house located on a floodplain? If so, what kind of insurance is required?
- □ Do you have water problems in the basement? (If so, you must show the buyer that you have rectified the problem.) Do you have warranties or guarantees on the work?
- □ Where are the local schools, and what is their quality? (You should know about such things as facilities, transportation, student-teacher ratios, special programs, and the percentage of students who go on to higher education.)
- □ What is the availability and cost of mass transit?
- □ Where are the places of worship in the area?
- □ What are the costs of joining the local golf course or country club?

Make available copies of your property survey and any pre-listing inspection or appraisal report. Also provide prospects with a list of recent major improvements to the property.

It may take time to gather all this information from old bills, tax statements, work receipts, service contracts, and warranty documents, but it pays off in the end. You will appear to have nothing to hide, and buyers will be reassured that your house is reasonable to maintain and keep up. Most important, you will be building a good relationship with buyers. Having all this information on hand also helps home inspectors who want to know the ages of the appliances in the home, and its major structural elements.

Place the marketing materials on a foyer table or the living room coffee table. At the end of the tour, invite likely prospects to discuss their needs and how your home might suit them. Don't be pushy, but take advantage of their expressed interest to further explain or clarify these matters.

You may not have the time to build the rapport that a real estate agent tries to cultivate with each client, so you'll need to size up each prospect's personality fairly quickly. If you do, you can shape the way you show your home to the individual buyer. For example, some prospects prefer to be guided through the home, chatting all the way. Others may choose to look on their own so they can comment freely regarding the home and its features.

NEGOTIATING WITH A BUYER

Initially, you may do most of your negotiating over the phone. The final offer should be in writing, however, or the agreement may not be enforceable. Once you and the buyer have agreed on a price and a closing date, both parties have a sales contract drawn up, preferably by a lawyer.

In fact, if you do sell your home without an agent, don't try to dispense with the services of an experienced real estate lawyer. Most banks and mortgage companies require a lawyer to review sales contracts, although in some states—California, for example—lawyers are not required. (In these states, however, there is almost always a broker as well as a title or escrow company that handles the paperwork.) Considering the number of documents that need to be reviewed, and the differing state requirements, it's always prudent to hire a lawyer to oversee the legal aspects of any sale.

Documents you need to provide include the *sales* or *purchase agreement, disclosure forms, escrow instructions, inspection certificates*, and *deeds*. There may also be a number of *contingency clauses* written into the purchase agreement by you, the buyer, or both parties (see chapter 13). If you agree to help the buyer with financing, legal counsel is imperative to make sure you are protected against default by the buyer.

The Down Payment and Other Deposits

Typically, after you have accepted a bid, the buyer pays 10 percent or less of the selling price to keep the home off the market while he or she seeks financing. In some areas, this "earnest-money" deposit may be as little as $1,000, and in some states, this initial "good faith" deposit becomes part of a 10-percent down payment due 10 days after contract signing, with the remainder due at closing. In other states, the escrow money that accompanies the offer simply becomes part of the down payment paid at closing.

This earnest money deposit should be placed into an escrow account until all issues are resolved regarding the contract, usually until the closing. The escrow account is held by a mutually acceptable third party, often an escrow company, but sometimes the seller's attorney. Your contract should specify the situations under which the buyer may forfeit the money. For example, the buyer may lose the deposit if the buyer reneges on the deal because of failure to find a buyer for his or her own home, or if the buyer finds a better house.

FINDING AN ATTORNEY

You can select a real estate attorney through referrals from friends and neighbors, by contacting a local bar association, or by asking a real estate agent for the names of at least three lawyers. Or use the *Martindale-Hubble Law Directory*, which is available at most public libraries.

Most state bar associations require that a lawyer carry malpractice insurance high enough to cover the price of the home, in the rare event that a buyer should sue an owner and try to back out of the transaction. Having this coverage is important to most lenders, because if a lawsuit does occur after the sale, the buyer can seek damages from the lawyer, not the seller or the mortgage provider.

7

Working with
a Real Estate Agent

The majority of homeowners sell their homes with the help of a real estate broker or agent. Real estate agents, also called salespeople or sales associates, work for and are representatives of a real estate broker. The broker employs the agent, and signs listings, approves changes to listing contracts, negotiates commissions, and makes decisions about special requests made by home sellers regarding listing periods or additional newspaper advertising.

A broker has a state license to own and operate an office, whereas an agent has a state license to sell property as an employee of a broker. Brokers and agents both must complete a course of classroom study and pass a state examination, but the educational requirements vary considerably from state to state.

The term *Realtor* is a registered trademark of the National Association of Realtors (NAR), an organization that has about 800,000 members. Anyone who calls himself or herself a realtor must belong to the NAR.

You may want to consider using a broker or agent if you've never sold a home before, or if you are selling in a slow market. An experienced agent can guide you through the selling process; the agent also does most of the work.

When you put your house on the market through an agent, make sure the agent is working for *you*, the seller, and not the buyer. The agent has a fiduciary duty (a position of trust) to get you the highest price for your home, and as quickly as possible. As of this writing, 44 states have laws requiring real estate agents to disclose to the seller *in writing* the parties they represent. Although in recent years there has been an increase in the number of brokers who work for the buyer, the vast majority of brokers and agents represent sellers. (Buyer brokers are more prevalent in the West and South than in the East.) If your agent or broker does not disclose this information to you, ask about it.

An agent who works for you, the seller, is ethically and legally bound to pass along any information a buyer has divulged that might benefit you during negotiations. Your agent also has a responsibility to let you know whether the buyer is willing to pay a certain amount for your property, or is willing to make concessions. Similarly, a buyer broker has a responsibility to use the information he or she learns from you to help the buyer strike a favorable deal. However, unless the buyer has a *written contract* with the broker stating that the broker owes duties only to the buyer, a broker or agent selected by the buyer may still legally owe duties to the seller.

If you are working with an agent other than the one who listed your home, or if you receive an offer from any broker or agent, make it your business to ask whether he or she represents you or the buyer. Unless the broker is a buyer broker, your inquiry will remind brokers and agents that legally they represent you, the seller, and you should get this in writing.

As a prudent seller, however, you should take the wisest course of action, which is to be careful what you say. Unless you know and trust the agent, don't mention how low you will go in price, or give away any information that could be harmful to your negotiating position. Of course, it's in the selling agent's best interest to see that a sale goes through at an acceptable price, so the agent should do everything reasonable to sell your property in a timely manner and solve problems to both parties' satisfaction.

Specifically, a competent selling agent should include the following steps in marketing your home:

- ☐ visit your property and take notes on its size, condition, and neighborhood
- ☐ research comparable properties and come up with a fair market value for your home
- ☐ suggest ways to improve your home's curb appeal and marketability
- ☐ inform you of state laws regarding disclosure of defects
- ☐ list your home in the local Multiple Listing Service, if there is one in your area
- ☐ draw up and discuss with you a marketing plan for your home
- ☐ write and place ads for your home in local newspapers
- ☐ recommend and implement creative marketing techniques, such as creating fact sheets and mailing notices to neighbors
- ☐ show your home to its best advantage
- ☐ advertise and host open houses for other brokers and buyers, and report the results to you
- ☐ screen prospective buyers to make sure they can afford your home
- ☐ suggest how to overcome any objections the prospective buyers may have

Before listing your home with a broker or agent, discuss with him or her the marketing steps to be undertaken, as well as the timing of these steps; ask that the broker or agent include a list of the steps and the time plan as part of the listing contract.

A selling agent who has listed your home is also expected to take the following steps during negotiations and at the closing:

- ☐ write up and present all offers and counteroffers and generally serve as a go-between during negotiations
- ☐ mediate disputes, suggest compromises, and help solve problems

- ☐ draw up the sales agreement in consultation with you
- ☐ ensure that escrow money is deposited properly
- ☐ help buyers find financing and get a mortgage
- ☐ ensure that contracts and other paperwork are completed correctly and according to legal requirements
- ☐ follow through on appraisals, inspections, the mortgage application, the escrow deposit and arrangements, warranties, disclosure forms, and contingencies of sale
- ☐ help you and the buyer find a home inspector and lawyer, if necessary, by providing a list of names
- ☐ attend the closing to make sure all goes smoothly, if necessary

THE MULTIPLE LISTING SERVICE

One of the most important advantages of listing your home with a real estate agent is access to the Multiple Listing Service (MLS). This computerized listing system gives agents from all participating brokers, who pay an annual fee to belong to the MLS, access to other brokers' listings. Even a small real estate firm that may have only a dozen listings of its own can still show many homes and attract many more buyers because of MLS access. (Buyer brokers may also be able to list your home on the MLS, but will charge you for the service.)

Even though agents give their own listings priority, they show other brokers' listings, especially to meet buyers' special needs.

Most agencies participate in the MLS, but make sure of this before you sign a listing contract. If you list your home exclusively with an agency that does not participate in the MLS, you will have far fewer agents trying to sell your home, and it will get much less exposure. Don't let a real estate broker talk you into waiting a number of weeks before he or she puts your home into the MLS, either; this ploy indicates that the broker is just looking for a bigger commission.

There are some 1,000 Multiple Listing Services in the United

States, and each has its own rules and operating procedures. In many areas, the MLS entries are printed in book form and updated frequently; some services update them daily. Organized by town and price, the MLS book contains photos, addresses, and descriptions of houses, including age, property size, number of rooms, type of heating, and property taxes, along with data on how long each home has been listed and what items are included and excluded in the sale.

THE OBLIGATIONS OF THE SELLER

The agent has responsibilities to you, but you also have some obligations to the agent. Your primary responsibility is to disclose problems and defects that are not apparent on a walk-through of your home, but you must also keep your home in showing condition, make it available for showings on short notice, allow the agent to take the lead in dealing with the buyers, negotiate in good faith, and generally assist by being cooperative and reasonable.

The important responsibility of disclosure comes first—from radon and asbestos to a wet basement or leaky roof. Agents are increasingly putting the onus on the seller to reveal these hidden problems. If you fail to do so, you risk being sued, in which case you may owe damages as well as having to pay the buyers the cost of making repairs. If you misrepresent a condition by stating there is no problem when in fact you know of its existence, you could be sued for misrepresentation. Today some real estate brokers will not accept a listing unless a disclosure form is signed by the seller at the time of the listing. A buyer can then review the form before making an offer.

You are also obligated to keep your home in showing condition every day. If you find it difficult to show your home on short notice because you are working a night shift, have small children, or are running a business out of your home, explain the situation to the agent. You can agree or compromise on the amount of advance notice you need, with the understanding that you may lose a few prospects as a result. It's better to resolve such problems *before* you enter into an agreement with an agent, so that neither party ends up having different expectations or wasting time with a relationship that turns out to be unproductive.

Try to leave the house when your agent brings buyers to see it. The buyers will feel more comfortable, and you won't be forced to overhear negative comments about your home. The agent will also be free to concentrate on the buyers' reactions, not yours. If you can't leave to run an errand or take a walk, make yourself inconspicuous and leave the talking to the agent.

Your absence is especially important if a prospect asks to see your home more than once. A repeat visit indicates serious interest, and buyers will be better able to discuss and examine your home at their ease if you are not there.

FINDING A REPUTABLE BROKER

A seller today can choose from a variety of types of brokerage firms: large national chains, regional brokers, midsize local brokers with several offices, or small local brokers with one or two offices. There are even referral services affiliated with larger regional or national brokerage networks that recruit licensed but generally inactive sales agents who function as members and who can refer to the networks' potential sellers or buyers. If the sale or purchase is completed through the agent selected by the service to handle the transaction, the referral agent receives a commission paid by the broker.

The National Association of Realtors classifies small brokerage firms as having up to 5 salespeople; large brokerage firms have more than 50. Although large companies make up only 3 percent of all agencies, they employ more than 50 percent of all sales agents. Small firms make up 52 percent of all agencies, but employ just 8 percent of all agents.

A large national chain may have thousands of outlets owned and operated by the parent company. Others are franchise operations in which different owners buy the right to establish individual

USING A LOCKBOX

Unless your home contains many valuables, or is in a high-crime area, consider having a lockbox (also called a keybox) installed by the agent. A lockbox attaches near the front or back door of your home, and holds a key to your house. It is kept locked and can be opened only by those agents with a key (i.e., the members of your local MLS). A lockbox gives agents more opportunities and greater freedom and flexibility in showing your home.

Because a few unscrupulous agents or others have used lockboxes for unlawful entry and theft, a number of real estate boards are switching to more expensive computer lockbox systems. To access these boxes, agents are given individual code numbers that are changed frequently; the computers will register who entered the residence and at what time.

In any case, remove and store valuables under lock and key during the time your home is on the market. You will avoid tempting buyers and agents and also prevent possible disputes in the event an expensive item disappears or gets misplaced.

offices in a specified area. Thirty-five percent of all agencies in the United States are affiliated with a regional or national organization.

Types of Brokers

There is no single right choice of realtor for everybody. You may prefer a small firm that has strong roots in your community and gives you personal attention. Small brokerage firms may also be more flexible about commissions. Free of bureaucracy and layers of staff, the small firm allows you the freedom and ease to talk and meet with the chief broker quickly and easily, to discuss problems or new ideas on marketing your home.

Often, a small brokerage has carved out a niche in its community to serve a particular type of home buyer (first-time, move-up, or ethnic group, for example) or sell a particular type of home. If you or your home falls into the category served by that broker, or you are a member of that ethnic group, you may feel more comfortable dealing with that broker.

Or perhaps you favor the resources offered by a large chain. These comprehensive realty firms offer special training and continuing education for their agents, may give relocation assistance to clients, feature special condo and co-op divisions, and have financial or mortgage specialists on staff who prequalify buyers and help them find financing. Some of these brokers provide television advertising, as well as magazines of company-listed homes, and printed and videotaped information on homes for sale in your area.

Larger firms may also furnish cellular phones for all of their agents so that they can be reached on the road, and audiotexts that allow buyers to listen to descriptions of homes for sale in their general price range.

Large firms can have their drawbacks, though. For example, it may be easier for an inexperienced agent to be hired at a large real estate sales office than at a small one. Large firms frequently place the newer agents on telephone duty; if you make a "cold call" to a large local realty office, you're likely to get one of the less experienced agents who has been assigned to answer any incoming calls. To avoid this, ask about a particular agent's experience, or seek referrals from friends and acquaintances so you can ask for a specific agent by name.

Most important, seek a firm that:

□ belongs to the Multiple Listing Service
□ sells many of the homes in your area, especially in your immediate neighborhood
□ advertises frequently, showing that it has the resources to draw buyers

- holds a state broker's license, which should be on display at the main office. Any branch offices should display a branch office license
- is a member of the National Association of Real Estate Brokers or the National Association of Realtors, both professional organizations that promote ethical behavior for their members and keep them current on changes in the real estate field

What to Do First

Before putting your home on the market, call or visit several brokers who have a good reputation in your area. Ask them what the procedure is for listing your home. First, the broker should offer to perform a comparative market analysis (see chapter 4), and he or she should show a genuine interest in the marketing of your home. The broker should also outline the steps necessary to market and sell your home. If the broker pressures you to sign a listing agreement on the spot, or before these steps are completed, go elsewhere.

Note how busy the offices seem, and how professionally the agents handle buyers in the office and over the phone. Agents should question buyers carefully on their preferences, and should patiently suggest different homes if buyers don't seem right for the ones advertised, or don't like the ones they've been shown.

Find out how well the agents know your town and whether they are familiar with your neighborhood. You want a broker who sells your type of home, in your area, in your price range. Does the broker specialize in a particular type of property, such as condos, estates, commercial property, or historic homes? If your home is a three-bedroom Cape Cod and the company sells mostly million-dollar properties, you may not get the attention you deserve, or the broker may fail to promote your home and fail to reach appropriate buyers.

Don't be satisfied with vague assurances about the firm's specialties and capabilities. The fact that an office specializes in a particular segment of the market does not tell you how capable an individual selling agent will be. Ask the agent who proposes to list your home how many similar homes he or she has sold in the last 12 months—not just the yearly amount of sales made by the firm.

SELECTING AN AGENT

When looking for an agent, too many sellers choose someone they personally know who is in the business—often a relative—or sign a brokerage agreement with the first agent who comes up with the highest suggested list price for their home. Neither method takes into consideration an agent's qualifications, abilities, experience, personality, or how hard the agent is likely to work to sell your home.

Selecting an agent on the basis of his or her estimated price for your home can actually be detrimental to a successful sale. First, the agent may suggest an unrealistically high price just to get your listing. This is especially true if you indicate you are looking for the most you can make on your home or if you have asked several agents to present you with competitive listing prices.

Second, some agents price high in order to earn a larger commission. This tactic may work in a market that is heading upward, but hurts a home's marketability in a depressed selling climate.

Third, some agents make their living primarily from collecting listings and then waiting for other agents to do the selling. Recommending a too-high price for a home is their usual method of operation. Once this type of agent gets your listing, little or nothing may be done to promote your property; the agent knows it's simply a matter of time until he or she collects a slice of the commission.

Finally, a listing price that's too high leads other agents to avoid bringing buyers to your home. Or your home may be shown primarily to allow the buyer to compare it to some other more realistically priced property.

Make it clear from the beginning that you will not choose an agent solely based on his or her notion of price. Tell the agents you interview that you want to sell your home within a reasonable time, and that you are looking for effective ideas on how to market it successfully.

Recommendations are, as always, among the best criteria for choosing an agent. Ask neighbors and friends who have sold their property recently about their agents. How quickly did the home sell? Did it sell at or close to its asking price? Homeowners who have been through a selling experience are usually eager to recommend a good performer or caution you against a poor one.

Another way to find a good agent is to scan the real estate sections of local newspapers and note the names of agents who are quoted as "experts" or who receive commendations for their sales volume or other achievements.

What to Look For in an Agent

In general, experience counts among real estate agents. An agent with at least four to five years' full-time experience has a roster of contacts (lawyers, termite services, mortgage companies), a list of past sellers who can serve as references, and a number of creative ideas about marketing your home.

To determine agents' familiarity with the local market and their ability to answer buyers' questions, ask agents how long they have been working on a full-time basis in your area. An agent who has recently moved to your town isn't likely to have the same firsthand knowledge as a more established agent, especially if you have questions about schools, communities, transportation systems, tax rates, and cultural attractions. Give an extra point or two to an agent who currently has listings in your area and has sold one or more homes in the past three months. Using a local agent rather than one working out of an office a few towns away means that the local agent can get to your home quicker when a buyer calls and wants to see it *now*. Also, the in-town agent is likely to know and be able to promote your town's advantages.

Hire an agent who works full-time. Buyers prefer full-time agents, who are usually available to show homes at almost any time, not merely as the agent's schedule allows.

Look for an agent who has sold homes in both cool and hot markets. In a strong market, a top agent sells about one home a month. In a weak market, the same agent might sell one home every two or three months. Of course, even a good agent may sell nothing for six months and then have two or three closings the next month, owing to luck and timing. The important figure to look at is the agent's *average* number of listings and sales over a period of time, not the agent's month-to-month track record.

It would be a mistake to eliminate new agents from the running, however; an efficient, smart, and creative newcomer may give your listing more time and attention than will a more experienced agent who is rushed and pressured, trying to serve many clients at once.

Ideally, you want someone who is enthusiastic, and whose personality complements your own. Remember, the agent should ask for your listing, but not pressure you. If the agent is pushy and doesn't take the time to discuss your needs or suggest marketing ideas, that may be a sign that he or she is a "listing collector," and not an active seller.

Comparing CMAs. One way to select an agent and test his or her savvy is to ask about the current market and how it affects selling strategy and price. The agent should be able to back up any assertions with proof. That proof might be in the form of newspaper articles, statistics from the local real estate board, or the selling prices of comparable properties.

Each agent should also present a sound argument and documentation on how he or she arrived at your home's proposed market value or price range. The comparative market analysis (CMA) should contain listing and selling prices, descriptions, and photos of comparable homes, and should reveal how long those houses have been on the market and whether any price cuts have been made. The agent should also explain how the differences between your property and the comparables affect your home's value.

An agent should ask your reasons for selling, the date you need to move, what improvements have been made to the property, and whether there are any defects or problems with the home. These questions will show that the agent is concerned with and responsive to your needs, which in turn will help dictate selling strategy.

Check References

Ask the agent for references from recent sellers. Chances are the agent will refer you only to clients who were happy with his or her services, but you can still ask some specific questions to help you determine the agent's competence, including these:

- ☐ Did the agent give you ideas on how to make your home more salable?
- ☐ How long was your home on the market?
- ☐ Do you think the agent priced it realistically?
- ☐ What did it sell for? What was the original listing price?
- ☐ How often was your home shown?
- ☐ What type of marketing did the agent do for your home?
- ☐ Did the agent fulfill all of his or her promises to you?
- ☐ Did the agent keep you informed of agents' and buyers' reactions to your home?
- ☐ How many offers did you get?
- ☐ Did the agent follow up on tasks that needed to be done for the closing?
- ☐ Was there anything the agent did that you didn't like?
- ☐ Would you use the agent for your next home sale?

COMMISSIONS

Real estate brokers' commissions are not set by law. The traditional fee in most parts of the country is 6 percent of the selling price, and brokers don't like to negotiate below this prevailing rate. You are legally entitled to negotiate for a lower rate, but the agent is not required to agree to it.

If you request a commission below 5 percent, some brokers may say that they do not want to list your property, claiming it is

WHAT TO EXPECT FROM AN AGENT

First, a competent real estate professional knows that he or she is working for you, the seller. This means the agent is intent on getting you the best price possible in the shortest possible time. In a slow market, the agent should present some creative ideas and strategies to highlight your property and attract buyers. Other promotional responsibilities include the following:

Marketing Plan. The agent should do more than just provide a physical description of your home to prospects. Instead, the agent should *sell* the benefits of your property, location, and area. Because you will be spending a considerable amount of money to have the broker and agent sell your home, you should expect a detailed, written marketing plan for you to review before you sign a listing contract. Then have the plan attached to the listing agreement and made a part of the contract.

Advertising. It's usually sufficient if an ad for your home is placed in local newspapers several times during the selling period. The truth is, though sellers take pride in seeing their homes advertised, these ads seldom sell particular homes. They are really selling tools for the broker; they show buyers that the broker lists certain types of homes in various price ranges, and help to keep the broker's name before the public. While the broker will ask you whether or not you want your house advertised, he or she will seldom allow a seller to approve advertising copy.

Open House. Agents may recommend holding an open house occasionally, perhaps once every six weeks, especially in a slow market. Ask the agent what will be done to promote the event, how long it should take, and what the agent hopes to gain by the event. If you don't want an open house, make that clear to the agent.

Buyer Showings. An experienced agent will screen buyers before bringing them to your home, and make sure that they are likely to qualify for adequate financing. The agent should have established connections with lenders and should know how to assist buyers in obtaining a mortgage. You should also expect the agent to give you adequate notice before bringing buyers to your home; an hour or two is reasonable. If you ask for more notice, however, agents may find it difficult to accommodate you, because buyers often drop in unexpectedly and many are in town only for the day to look at properties.

Keeping You Informed. Much of seller dissatisfaction with real estate agents occurs when agents fail to keep the seller informed of developments. Stress that you want to hear from the agent once a week or every two weeks about the progress of the sale, and more often if there is an interested buyer in the picture.

not worth the cost involved. If you do negotiate a lower commission, there is a risk that agents may steer buyers to more profitable listings.

Moreover, the widespread use of the MLS gives agents a choice of hundreds of full-commission properties to sell, and makes it likely that your listing broker will have to absorb the full loss in revenue of a lowered commission. Obviously, most brokers are not enthusiastic about lowering their commission rates, but you should shop around for the best deal you can find, including using discount brokers (see chapter 6).

You also have additional bargaining power with agents if you are using them to sell your existing home as well as to find you a new residence. An agent will not receive a commission on either home unless the existing home is sold, so he or she has a strong incentive to push your house even if it will earn a reduced selling commission.

Selling Through the Multiple Listing Service

It's important that you, as the seller, understand how the commission system operates and how the listing agent and broker make their money. Ask the agent to outline clearly for you the various procedures and compensations that occur when a sale goes through the Multiple Listing Service.

The most common scenario is that your home is listed by one real estate broker and then sold by another. The two firms split the commission, usually 50-50 but sometimes 60-40 in favor of the selling broker. Each part of the commission is split again between listing agent and listing broker, and selling agent and selling broker. So, on a $200,000 sale with a 6-percent commission of $12,000, your listing agent might take home $3,000; if the listing agent also sells the home, his or her commission increases to $6,000.

At 100-percent-commission firms, agents pay brokers a set monthly fee for overhead, but split their commissions only with the other selling or listing agent, not with the broker. If the same agent both lists and sells the property, he or she keeps the entire commission. These firms usually charge the seller a slightly lower commission.

Reducing the Commission. You may find that smaller real estate firms are more receptive to negotiating commissions. Some may even position themselves as discount brokers, and require you to do some of the work of selling your home, such as showing it yourself. These firms charge a set fee or a sliding fee based on the price of the home, which is often half that of standard commissions. Discount brokers are not found as readily during a weak market, however, because discounters suffer when homes require more intense marketing and thus cost more to sell.

There are other ways to try to reduce the commission. Perhaps you don't care about newspaper or TV advertising, open houses, or other creative selling techniques; you may be satisfied with only a listing in the MLS and a sign on your front lawn. If you can accept a reduction in service, the broker may be more inclined to accept a lower commission. Just make sure you don't lose any vital services in return for paying the discounted rate. In a slow market, you may find paying the full commission worth the cost if it helps sell your home faster and at a reasonable price.

You are more likely to be successful in negotiating a lower commission when you own an expensive home, because the broker and agent will be earning a large commission on its sale and so will be more amenable to a lower percentage of the price. Other reasons may be if your home is in excellent condition or located in a highly desirable area.

You may want to think twice about whether to cut the broker's commission in a soft market when your home is competing with many others. If you do, agents have less incentive to sell your home. And the longer your home sits on the market, the less significant will be any potential savings from a reduced commission, owing to the increased costs of maintenance and taxes. If you agree to sell your home and buy another through the broker, however, you may be able to negotiate a lower commission.

If a buyer offers the full asking price for your home, you are legally obligated to go through with the transaction and pay the full commission as set forth in your listing agreement. On the other hand, agents may give up a small part of their commission if it helps resolve a difficult negotiation.

Buyer brokers, those agents who aid the buyer in the purchase of a home, are paid by the buyer at an hourly rate of $50 to $140, or they collect a percentage of the home's selling price, usually about 3 percent. If you are approached by a buyer broker who wants to show your home to a client, make sure you understand clearly how the buyer broker is paid, and by whom.

LISTING AGREEMENTS

The listing agreement is a contract in which you promise a commission to the real estate broker and agent who finds a qualified buyer for your property. The buyer must meet certain terms and conditions, such as offering a price that is acceptable to you.

The listing agreement must be dated and include the address, the block and lot number from your property survey or title policy, and a full description of the property. It also includes the listing price, the rate of commission for the broker, any special terms or contingencies, and the expiration date of the listing. The agreement must be signed by both the firm's authorized broker and the owners of the property, and the agent must furnish you with a fully executed copy. Make sure the listing agreement contains the following language: "No commission shall be due or payable unless and until the closing on the sale actually occurs."

Many agents hand you their standard listing agreement at the end of their presentation and ask you to sign it, often without explaining all your options. Take the time to review the exact nature of your agreement with them, and explore the other kinds of listing agreements that are available.

Types of Listing Agreements

The three most common listing agreements are the *exclusive right to sell*, the *exclusive agency listing*, and the *open listing*.

Exclusive Right to Sell. In this type of agreement, you give the listing broker the sole right to sell your property for a stated period, usually a few months. Other brokers can work to sell the home, but no matter who sells or leases the property during that period—another broker or even you—the listing broker receives a commission. If another broker sells the property, he or she splits the commission with the listing broker. This type of contract is required by most real estate boards for a property to be listed on the MLS.

Exclusive Agency Listing, or Nonexclusive Listing. This agreement carries the same rights as the exclusive listing except that you reserve the right to sell the home yourself, without having to pay a commission to the listing broker. Other brokers can still cooperate on selling the property and receive a share of the commission. Some real estate boards allow properties with exclusive agency listings to be entered into the MLS.

Open Listing. Here the entire commission is paid to the broker who makes the sale. This contract gives the right to sell the property to all brokers, but stipulates that a commission will be paid to the first agent who presents an offer that meets a specified price and terms. No agent is given an exclusive right to sell in an open listing.

You can sign open-listing contracts with as many brokers as you wish, with the same or different expiration dates. As with the exclusive agency listing, you can reserve the right to sell your property yourself and not be obligated to pay a commission to any broker. Unlike the other two types of listings, however, this listing *cannot* be put on the Multiple Listing Service.

Other Listing Options

Brokers generally push for the exclusive listing; otherwise they believe they may waste time and money promoting a listing that you then sell on your own. You may be able to negotiate for the exclusive agency listing if the market in your area has many buyers but is low on listings, or if you agree to give the broker a small commission even if you do sell on your own.

Many brokers insert a protection clause in the exclusive and exclusive agency listings. It states that if the home is sold after the listing expires to a buyer who first saw the property with a real estate agent during the term of the listing, you owe the listing broker the full commission. This clause is designed to prevent owners and buyers from conspiring to eliminate the broker's commission, usually by waiting until the listing expires before they proceed with a sale. You should negotiate this clause with your broker if the time period following the expiration of the listing is excessively long (more than three months). Also, the broker should be required to list all the prospects that have seen the home and for whom he or she seeks protection.

Another type of listing agreement found in a few states, but illegal in most, is the *net listing*. Here you agree to receive a minimum acceptable net amount from the sale, with the broker getting any additional payment above that. For example, you might tell the broker, "I want $200,000 for my house; if you sell it for more, you can keep the balance." A net listing gives an unscrupulous agent a good reason to underprice your home, and an opportunity to earn a great deal of money as a result of your—or the buyer's— inexperience and trust. Avoid this type of listing; it serves only the agent and broker, not you.

In most states, listing agreements are not enforceable unless they are in writing. Even in those few states where oral agreements are accepted, the broker is usually advised to put the agreement in writing for his or her protection. If you don't negotiate the terms of the agreement, the broker has a strong case for collecting a commission.

Once you sign a listing agreement with a broker or a broker's agent, you owe a commission if a "ready, willing, and able" buyer agrees to purchase your home *at the full listing price* within the specified time. You may decide at that time not to sell your home after all, but you may still owe a commission. You can protect yourself against this possibility by negotiating a provision in the listing agreement that permits you to withdraw your home from the market at any time and not be obligated to pay a commission unless the sale goes through and a closing occurs. Check out the listing agreement carefully to determine your obligations *before* you sign it.

Ask the agent or broker how offers will be presented to you. To reduce chances of a misunderstanding, official offers should be made in person by the listing agent or by the selling agent with the listing agent present. Also insist on having all offers, no matter how low, presented to you.

Listing Agreement Stipulations

Discuss the terms you want with the agent and be sure that the changes or additions you want are made to the listing contract. Most agreements give the broker authority to distribute your listing to members of the Multiple Listing Service. Ask how long it will take to enter your property in the MLS; it should generally be done within a few days. Each MLS has its own requirements, however. If you do not want your home listed on the MLS (some sellers want only one agent to show their home), let your listing agent know, and include that in the contract. Or if you are particularly concerned about security, you may decide not to have a lockbox installed.

Ask your agent to attach the marketing plan to your listing contract. The plan should detail what will be done to advertise, market, and otherwise promote your home to potential buyers. It should state when and how often your home will be listed in the MLS system, when and where advertisements will be placed, when the For Sale sign will go up, and approximately how often the agent will hold an open house. The contract itself should state that the agent will implement the marketing plan.

Don't agree to any special buyer concessions at this time. For example, don't make generous offers in the listing agreement regarding owner financing or items you will include with the sale; you can always change your mind later on.

If there are certain hours, such as dinnertime, or days when you don't want buyers touring your home, specify that in the listing contract. Repeated failure to respect these conditions, or others written into the agreement, can be grounds for you to cancel the contract and change agents.

The *term* of your listing agreement depends on the market. In a buyer's market, homes typically take more than 90 days to sell, and many agents won't take listings for fewer than six months. The agent and broker know that the chances of selling the home diminish with a shorter period, and the investment in selling your property probably won't be recouped.

In a strong market, homes typically sell within 60 days, sometimes much faster. Most listings run 60 to 120 days, with the average selling in 90 days. If you want to put pressure on your agent to sell quickly in a hot market, ask for a listing agreement of 60 days. At the end of that period, if the agent hasn't performed as expected, you are free to find a new agent. If you are satisfied with the agent's efforts, you can sign an extension of the listing agreement as many times as you wish, for as few as 30 days at a time.

In a weak market, however, you may not have the leverage with agents to insist on a short listing agreement. If you find the right agent, it may be to your advantage to agree to a longer listing—three to six months—with the written provision that you can back out of the agreement with 30 days' notice if you are not happy with the agent's performance. Never sign a listing agreement for a period longer than six months.

If you do not renew a listing agreement and someone who has seen your home during the listing period buys it within 90 days of the agreement's expiration, you generally must pay the agent's commission—depending on whether such a clause is in your agreement.

The listing agreement also stipulates when buyers can take possession of your home. While 60 to 90 days is typical, it's best to specify that the time is negotiable, if you are unsure about your future plans. You'll give yourself a marketing edge by not ruling out the possibility that a buyer may be able to take possession sooner or later than the standard period.

Always insist on reviewing the write-up for your home before it gets circulated to cooperating agents on a listing sheet and distributed via the MLS. The copy is prepared from information that you have provided. Check that the listing is accurate, the description complete, the correct fixtures specified, and any special instructions included for agents who show your home (such as calling for appointments or showing during certain hours only). The listing sheet should also give clear directions to your home. If any relevant facts change—such as taxes—or an error is made in the listing, it can be revised at any time. Some changes, such as a reduction in price, must be approved by both the broker and the seller.

Take a good look at the photo that will be included on the listing sheet and published in the MLS. If the photo is not flattering, insist that a new one be taken. Attractive photos and accurately written descriptions are critical to the successful marketing of your home.

Protecting Yourself

You may insist on adding a clause to the listing contract that allows you to renege on a sale and not owe a commission under specific circumstances. If you are worried that in the future you might have to back out of a sale, have your lawyer review the listing contract *before* you sign it, and make suggestions on how you can be protected.

There are legitimate reasons for not paying a commission. For example, you don't owe a commission if the buyer cannot get financing within the time frame stated in the contingency clause. Or you may have a family crisis, such as grave illness, death, divorce, or job loss that precludes your selling the home. In that case the broker should release you from the listing contract, although some may insist you pay for any out of pocket advertising expenses. If your broker refuses to agree to your request in such a situation, contact the local real estate board.

DIFFICULTIES WITH AGENTS AND BROKERS

Sometimes an agent turns out to be incompetent or behaves unethically. Such behavior can range from failure to promote your property or communicate with you to acting for more than one party in a transaction without the knowledge of all parties.

You have several options should these difficulties arise. First, speak with your agent. The agent may not be aware that you are unhappy or that you believe he or she is not performing adequately.

Maybe a personal problem has temporarily interfered with his or her work. Or buyer traffic may be low, not because of your agent's laziness, but owing to a too-high price, a lack of curb appeal, a slow time of year, or a bad market. For some reason, your agent may have been reluctant to discuss these problems with you.

Often the problems can be rectified with open communication and discussion about possible solutions. Or perhaps your agent *is* at fault and needs to know it. Tell your agent why you are not satisfied and what you would like to see changed.

If the agent agrees to correct the problem, give him or her one more chance over the course of another month to rectify the situation. Or the agent may voluntarily let you out of the listing agreement, realizing that an unhappy customer is detrimental to his or her reputation and business.

If the agent is uncooperative, explain that you will speak to the listing broker, and do so. You should get a satisfactory response, because the broker wants to preserve his or her company's reputation and potential for referral business.

If your broker is not helpful, seek recourse through your state's real estate commission or division of real estate by filing a written complaint. Before you do so, send a letter to your agent and broker notifying them of your intentions. That may solve the problem; no agent wants to be named in a complaint, and the agent or broker may take immediate steps to remedy the situation.

Real estate commissions should take customer complaints seriously. They will investigate an agent's or broker's actions, although it may take months to reach a resolution. If the agent is found to have committed an offense, his or her license can be suspended or revoked, or a fine imposed.

MAKING SURE YOUR AGENT
DOES A GOOD JOB

Close to 20 percent of home sellers change real estate agents while their property is still on the market. To avoid problems with your real estate agent, take these steps:

□ Choose an agent based on recommendations from friends or neighbors. They should have actually used that agent to sell a home, or know someone else who was pleased with the agent's performance.

□ Check the agent's references.

□ Ask for a detailed marketing plan before you list with the agent, and make it part of your listing agreement.

□ Listen to and follow your agent's advice, especially regarding repairing, pricing, and showing your home.

□ Ask your agent to call you with progress reports each week, and right after open houses.

□ Add a clause to your listing contract that gives you the right to back out with 30 days' notice.

□ Do not sign any listing agreement for longer than six months.

8

Selling in
a Slow Market

In a buyer's market—or anytime when you're having trouble selling your home—you need to do extra work to attract a buyer. Some steps involve spending money or making price concessions; still others mean adopting creative marketing techniques. Ideally, you take these actions before you list your home in order to achieve a quick sale. But you can also implement them later on if your home fails to sell.

IF YOU CAN'T SELL

When you are not getting buyer traffic or offers, ask your agent why, or—if you're selling on your own—make follow-up phone calls to prospects to find out their reactions. Certain situations may be hindering a successful sale, including problems with the property, drawbacks with the neighborhood, overpricing, or an ineffective selling broker or agent.

Problems with the Property

Perhaps a lack of curb appeal, interior defects, poor conditions, or property flaws are limiting interest. Maybe there's a dilapidated fence that needs repairing, too many trees, a swampy area that could be filled in or graded to drain properly, or noise from the road that could be deadened with a fence or landscaping.

Do an informal survey among neighbors and friends, asking them to give you an honest assessment of your home and property. They can be more objective than you can, and most will have some thoughts about what needs to be changed. Give priority to any problem or improvement that is mentioned more than once.

Unusual colors, for example, create a negative first impression that is hard to overcome. Houses painted or sided in unusual or outdated colors do not sell easily. Some colors, such as dark purple or lime green, are almost always unattractive. Others, such as pink or lavender, look fine in parts of the West and Florida, but are out of place on a Colonial or split-level. Repaint or, if necessary, re-side your home. If your home has other unusual or unattractive features, consider whether they can be eliminated, deemphasized, or changed.

Don't overlook the yard and landscaping; a paved-over backyard can be dug up and planted with seed or sod fairly inexpensively; a broken or gravel front walkway can be repaired or replaced with flagstones, bricks, or tinted and patterned concrete.

Except for repainting or re-siding, don't spend more than a couple of thousand dollars on cosmetics; adding imported granite countertops or tiled backsplashes featuring custom artwork is a waste of money. Stick to the basics, since buyers may not like your taste or may not appreciate expensive materials. The main tips to remember are to paint inside and out, make all needed repairs, freshen up landscaping, and clean thoroughly.

Drawbacks with the Neighborhood

Are there potholes in your street, or are you near an overgrown vacant lot?

If something about your neighborhood is bothering buyers, you may be able to correct the problem or at least improve the situation. Of course, a nearby industrial plant or a foul-smelling landfill or river can't be changed. But eyesores such as an empty lot, a neglected traffic island, a pothole-riddled street, or a rundown playground can be improved, with the cooperation of your neighbors. Point out to them how fixing the problem—either by soliciting your town to appropriate funds, collecting donations from residents, or volunteering labor—will benefit everyone by making the street a more attractive place to live and thereby increasing everyone's property values.

Overpricing

If buyers' and agents' reactions to your home are favorable, but you are not receiving offers or are getting only low bids, your price may be too high. If you are serious about selling, you will have to reduce your expectations. Price reductions do work; people like to feel they are getting a bargain, and the new selling price will bring in new buyers and agents. It may also stimulate previous lookers to make an offer. If it's any comfort, you will save some money on commission costs as well.

How much you choose to lower the price, and how long you should wait before doing so, depends on your home's general price range, how quickly you want to sell, the state of the market, and how realistic the price was originally.

If you set a price that was 15 or 20 percent higher than your home's market value, you must drop your price more than if you priced it only 5 percent higher. This is especially true if the market has deteriorated or if your need to move has become more pressing. Some sellers choose to cut the price in small increments several times over a period of months. Unless your home is priced below $100,000, this strategy can be harmful, chiefly because a home sitting on the market for a long time becomes "stale." It's better to make fewer and larger price cuts that attract attention, show you're serious about selling, and make an immediate difference in the ability of buyers to afford your home.

If homes in your area take approximately four to six months to sell, and your home's carrying costs are high, it makes financial sense to reduce your price only once, substantially, to sell it quickly. *Example:* Your carrying costs for four months total $16,000. Cutting the price $10,000 may get you an immediate sale, and you will come out ahead $6,000.

So, as a rule of thumb, if your home is priced at no more than $200,000 but above $100,000, cut $5,000 off the price. For homes priced below $100,000, cut $2,000 to $3,000. If your home is priced between $200,000 and $500,000, go for bigger incremental cuts of $10,000 to $15,000, or possibly more.

If the lower price still doesn't attract offers, you'll have to reduce the price again in another month or two. *Any home will sell if the price is low enough.* But you have to decide how low you are willing to go. If you will lose money on the sale, based on what you paid for the home, and will not make up that loss through equal or greater savings on a trade-up home, you may prefer to sit tight and wait for a buyer (or a better market) than cut your price any further.

Ineffective Selling Broker or Agent

If you're selling on your own, you can judge the effectiveness of your marketing by the number of inquiries you receive. If you receive very few, check that your ad is complete and highlights your home's strong points. Or rewrite the ad. Circulate different versions so buyers won't become too familiar with the house and wonder why it's on the market so long.

If you're selling with the help of an agent, you have an idea of how many buyers are visiting your home by the number of calls you get from agents wanting to set up appointments, the number of business cards that agents leave for you, and what your agent tells (or doesn't tell) you. If the agent is avoiding you, or you rarely get a request for an appointment, ask why. The reasons may be related to problems with the house or the neighborhood or the price, as discussed above. Or perhaps it's simply a soft market, and you need to be more patient.

Still, this is the time to ask your agent to produce evidence of what has been done to market your home—your MLS write-up and photo, any ads about your home, a fact sheet—and ask the agent to increase your home's exposure in the marketplace. If you see no signs of stepped-up activity within the next month, try to resolve the problem, switch agents, or sell on your own.

Once you resolve the obvious problems hindering your home's marketability, you can offer extra incentives to buyers and agents, and use other marketing tools that give your home a competitive edge to help it sell faster.

CREATIVE MARKETING STRATEGIES

When the market is slow or you're in a hurry to sell, look for agents with creative ideas and aggressive sales tactics that go beyond the standard practices. An enterprising agent can contact neighbors within a certain radius to let them know your home is available— for example, to suggest that their friends or relatives may be interested in the area. Your agent can make personal visits to these prospects, or distribute or mail a letter and information sheet, rather than just sending a card.

The agent can also take advantage of other brokers' and agents' open houses by *piggybacking*—that is, holding an open house for your property on the same day and at the same time, and making an agreement with the other agents to direct visitors to one another's open houses.

If the brokerage firm you are using is a large one, it may be able to offer more expensive marketing tools, such as listing your home in a directory arranged by town and price range, videotaping it for special buyer videos, or listing it in home guides published in different languages. There may be opportunities to show it on cable television programs, too. Or perhaps the brokerage can furnish you with special For Sale signs that invite drivers to tune in to a specified channel for radio-broadcast information about your home. These marketing resources make it easier for prospects to hear about your home and can help capture "impulse" buyers. Although it's important to choose a broker based on his or her knowledge, experience, and track record, in a down market it's best to give more weight to those who offer extra services and use aggressive selling techniques.

Before deciding on these services, however, ask the brokers whether a particular marketing tactic really sells homes. Don't settle for a quick yes; ask for proof.

Other potentially successful techniques that you can employ yourself are *warranties, selling to a broker or developer*, and *offering various incentives* for agents, brokers, and buyers.

Home Warranties

Offering a home warranty to a buyer can help close a sale. Warranties appeal especially to first-time buyers who are financially strapped and nervous about future maintenance bills.

During the first year of ownership, a home warranty policy guarantees to pay for repairs on appliances and electrical systems and sometimes plumbing and heating systems, once a deductible is met. Warranties also help protect the seller and broker against lawsuits by the buyer if appliances or systems break down after the closing.

A home warranty is a particularly good selling tool for an older home with more worn appliances and systems, or for any home that needs work or is poorly maintained. Sellers of older homes with known problems may have to pay a higher premium or have certain systems excluded from the warranty.

A number of real estate firms, lenders, home inspectors, and other companies (but *not* insurance companies) offer home warranties. One national real estate franchise, Electronic Realty Associates (ERA), pioneered the concept and offers its own program. Usually warranties cover a period of one year from the date of closing, but some also cover the home during the listing period. Companies generally sell warranties through real estate agents, not directly to sellers. People selling on their own, however, may be able to obtain a warranty (see below). A few brokers even pay for them themselves because they believe warranties are an important selling incentive.

As the seller, you do not pay for the warranty unless and until your home is sold. The typical cost of a one-year home warranty ranges in price from $325 to $400, and the average deductible is $100.

There are other kinds of home protection incentives for buyers, including your paying warranty costs on the appliances in the home, or paying the buyer's first year of homeowner's insurance. A home inspector may also offer a warranty based on an inspection report.

An inspection report and warranty coverage are two strong marketing tools that may convince buyers that your home is a prudent investment, if only because it is unlikely they will have to meet unexpected repair expenses in the future.

Selling to a Broker or Developer

If you can't sell on your own or with an agent, you may be able to find a local broker to buy your home, often at below-market value. ERA (see the preceding section on home warranties) offers such a program, called the Seller Security Plan. The program offers you the option, at the time of listing, to enter into an agreement that calls for the house to be sold to ERA at a preset price if the house does not sell on the open market after a 210-day period. However, you must close on the purchase of a new home through an ERA-designated broker by that time.

Before planning to take this option, you'll have to wait for your listing term to expire with your current agent. You will also need to check out carefully the terms and price available through a brokerage that offers such a home-buying service. At ERA, you pay for one appraisal and ERA pays for a second. ERA then offers you the price it will pay *before* a listing agreement is signed. If you accept ERA's offer, you agree to pay a commitment fee at the time of cancellation, equity advance, or closing. When ERA resells your

FINDING OUT ABOUT WARRANTIES

Ask your real estate agent to help you find a home warranty that meets your needs. Agents can contact the National Home Warranty Association, c/o Homeowners Marketing Services, Inc., P.O. Box 9200, Hollywood, FL 33084, for information on buying a policy. FSBO sellers can send a self-addressed, stamped envelope to the National Home Warranty Association, P.O. Box 12038, Marina del Rey, CA 90295. Ask for a list of companies that are members of the association, and the association's brochure "A Guide to Home Warranties for Consumers and Real Estate Professionals." The NHWA follows a professional code of ethics and upholds established standards of practice for the home warranty industry.

Make sure the company you select has a toll-free number and 24-hour service in case of an emergency. Check which appliances and systems are covered and whether there are dollar limits on payments per appliance or system.

If you decide to offer buyers a warranty, advertise "home warranty" or "home warranty protection" on your yard sign and in your flier and advertising.

home, any net gain minus sales and holding expenses is reimbursed to you. Any loss is absorbed by ERA. In 1991, 500 applications were made for the plan out of 250,000 transactions.

Understand your rights, obligations, and the terms of your contract before you enter into any agreement to sell your home to a broker. Such a plan merits consideration if you must sell quickly or need the equity from your home to move. In return, you must be willing to accept a price that is probably lower than the market value of the property, and perhaps pay other additional fees.

Selling to a Developer. If you want to buy a home in a new development, inquire if the builder will purchase your old home in return for your commitment to buy one of the units. Assuming you're moving up, you pay the difference between the two home prices. The builder may offer a discounted price for your property, but if you haven't been able to sell through conventional routes, it may be your best offer—and a way to move into the home you want. In a slow market, there are many anxious developers eager to sell their homes, and you will probably get a brand-new home at an even greater price reduction.

If the builder refuses to buy your home, he or she might at least agree to a sale that is conditional on the sale of your present home. This contingency allows you to back out of the contract if you ultimately can't sell your home. When sales are slow, developers are far more willing to consider such arrangements.

Incentives for Agents

In a soft market, some agents may ask for higher commissions or bonuses in return for working harder to sell your home. Typical bonuses run from $1,000 to $2,000, but some agencies ask for more. For homes priced in the million-plus range, some anxious sellers offer bonuses as high as $50,000.

For the average-priced home, it may help to offer an agent a commission one or two percentage points higher than the standard in your area. Usually the extra 1 percent goes to the selling broker. If an extra 2 percent is offered, the additional commission may be split between the listing and selling brokers, or all of it may go to the selling broker. The brokers then decide whether to split the extra commission with the listing or selling agent or give the agents the full amount. A bonus commission offer can be conditional on selling the home within a specified length of time, or it can run the duration of your listing contract.

You can specify that you will pay more—say, 8 percent—if your home is sold within a month or two. This gives agents an incentive to sell your home when it is fresh on the market and likely to attract the most attention. An extra 2-percent commission on a $200,000 home is $4,000 over the usual amount, but it may be worth it if you would otherwise be paying two mortgages for several months. Ask your agent if listings offering a higher commission have sold faster than equivalent standard-commission listings. If not, agreeing to pay a higher commission does not seem worthwhile.

For a bonus or higher commission to work, your home must be realistically priced. Otherwise, agents face too big a stumbling block to selling your home, and aren't willing to put in the extra work required. Bonuses and extra fees work best for unusual and expensive homes, those that have been on the market for a long time, or sellers who need to find a buyer fast.

In any case, if you do offer a bonus or large commission, select a top agent who has demonstrated an ability to sell your kind of home in a weak market. He or she should be a hard worker with creative marketing ideas, an aggressive marketing plan, and the willingness to spend time and money promoting your home.

Incentives for Buyers

Next to a reduced price, buyers respond best to offers of cash and help with financing their purchase (see chapter 9). Giveaways, such as trips, tickets to special events, gift certificates, and the like rarely motivate prospects to buy a home. These incentives may, however, get you some publicity and bring in more buyers. Someone who wasn't necessarily in the market for a home could read or hear about your offer, then become interested in the property. If you do offer an incentive, make sure your agent promotes it in any advertising and networking he or she does for your listing. And ask the agent to send out a notice to other brokers announcing the offer.

Offer gifts that are readily available and relatively inexpensive to give. For example, if you are moving and would be left with a car or boat in good condition that you no longer need, an expensive cedar swing set (for buyers with children), a transferable membership to a country club or swim club, a time-share at a nearby resort area you haven't been able to sell, or season tickets to a local football team or a concert series, offer to include those items in the sale of your home.

The price of such giveaways may range from a few hundred dollars to less than $10,000, except for a time-share, which might have cost you $20,000 to $30,000 when you purchased it. Still, given the notoriously poor resale market for time-shares, you can afford to add one to the purchase price. The primary advantage of offering an incentive versus cutting your price is that incentives are usually perceived by the buyer as costing more than they do, and they can generate excitement over a property. They may be something you don't particularly need or want anyway.

Don't tack on the costs of giveaways to the price of your home, though; most buyers will resent it. In fact, a buyer may ask for price concessions equal to the cost of the gift. It's to your advantage to negotiate, because the point of a bonus is mainly to attract a buyer who will make an offer for your home. Then you can negotiate how much you will discount the price of the home if the buyer doesn't want the gift after all. Your goal is to attract the buyer first, then work out the details later.

THE VACANT HOME

It's a fact of life that furnished homes sell faster than empty ones. Part of the reason is aesthetics: a furnished home looks more comfortable and appealing and helps buyers visualize themselves living in the house. Another reason is psychological: the buyer often gets the impression that a vacant house is a hard-to-sell house. If you must leave your present home before you sell it, taking all or most of the furnishings, make some attempt to give your vacant home a lived-in look.

One solution is to rent furniture, preferably from a store with a designer or decorator on staff to help you make the right selections. Some stores charge a fee for the services of a decorator, others don't. Take into account other expenses too, such as pickup and

HOW TO DRESS UP A VACANT HOME

If you decide to furnish your vacant home with rental items, professional decorators who design model rooms and homes suggest that you add a few personal touches:

- ☐ Set the dining room table as for a formal dinner.
- ☐ Put some brightly painted wooden toys or stuffed animals on top of a table or dresser in a nursery or child's bedroom.
- ☐ Place some books and magazines on the coffee table in the living room.
- ☐ Set attractive canisters on a kitchen counter.
- ☐ Add green plants (artificial ones can be quite attractive) to soften an empty corner and make the house seem lived in.
- ☐ Leave fresh towels and guest soap in the bathrooms.

delivery charges, security deposits, and insurance. Depending on the quality of the furniture you select and where you live, expect to pay $100 to $400 to furnish a living room, for example.

You don't need to rent too much furniture—only the basic pieces for each room, along with some area rugs, lamps, throw pillows, artwork, and a few accessories. The goal is to make the place look comfortable, attractive, and spacious.

A cheaper and better solution for most sellers is to hire a house-sitter, or home manager, who will furnish and live in the home and be prepared to vacate it on short notice. Having someone live in your home also deters vandals and reduces insurance rates, which can increase markedly if a home is left vacant.

You can find a house-sitter either through word of mouth or local advertising, but because of the risk in bringing a stranger into your home, you may feel more comfortable using the services of professional managers hired through residential management services. Two such companies are Showhomes of America (phone 214-243-1900) and Caretakers of America (phone 303-233-2676). These services screen house-sitters, who generally apply for the program as a result of financial difficulties. Sitters are matched to homes according to their geographic preferences and the style of their furniture, which must look attractive and blend in with the home's design.

House-sitters pay the utility and maintenance costs and must carry a limited liability insurance policy. They are also obligated to keep a home clean and to take care of any maintenance problems. They must agree to make the home available for showing 12 hours a day, seven days a week, and to vacate it in a matter of days. In return, the house-sitters are charged a rent that is 25 to 50 percent below market. The residential management company collects the rent as its fee.

Most homes that are manager-occupied sell in about 90 days, half the time it takes to sell an empty home. In addition, the average offer for an occupied home is at least 10 percent higher than for a vacant one.

TAX ASSESSMENTS

High taxes on a home can frighten away buyers, especially if the assessments seem out of line with those on similar homes in the same area. Of course, if your town's taxes are high, you or your agent has to explain that fact to a prospect and list what services or advantages are offered in return. For example, perhaps your town is mostly residential and the lot sizes are large and private. Residents may have just financed a new library. The town may boast a top-notch school system or several cultural attractions. In towns with high taxes, sellers must compensate by pricing homes somewhat lower than in a similar town with more reasonable taxes.

Of course, if you think your property taxes are too high, file an appeal to get them lowered. More than half of homeowners who challenge their assessments end up with lower tax bills. If you own a condominium, and condo prices have dropped more than home prices in your area, you probably have a good case for an appeal. Since there is strength in numbers, condo owners living in a large development should pursue tax appeals on a cooperative basis.

Also find out whether your town assesses taxes at full value or fractional value. If your town uses a 50-percent assessment, for example, and the fair market value of your home is $200,000, your home's assessed value should be $100,000. If it is higher, find out why. Perhaps the tax appraiser made a mistake in figuring your home's square footage, or listed your home as having a two-car garage when it does not, or incorrectly assumed an unheated summer porch was a heated room. Such mistakes can be fixed easily by checking the property record form at the town assessor's office.

If no simple error is uncovered, you can then file an appeal yourself or hire a certified appraiser or property tax consultant to do it for you. Consultants usually have excellent track records in winning their cases, but they may charge 50 percent or more of your first-year savings.

Another reason to file an appeal is if your home has declined in value because of a change in its condition or that of the neighborhood. You may have just discovered serious termite damage or a sinkhole in your backyard, for example. Perhaps your town has become a less desirable place to live as the result of water or air pollution caused by a nearby industrial plant. Maybe the house on the corner lot next door was torn down and a convenience store put up in its place.

Your case may be more complex and less clear-cut. You may disagree with your home's declared market value based on a decline in your area's home prices since the last appraisal. Or you may believe neighbors with similar houses pay less in taxes than you do. You have to support your contentions with documentation in the form of comparables from real estate agents, a professional appraisal, or careful research on similar homes that have recently sold in your neighborhood. If you lose your first appeal, you can solicit your county's tax board for relief.

9

Offering Financing to Buyers

□

The most popular type of incentive you can offer buyers in a slow market, next to reducing the price, is buyer financing. This can include the following:

□ helping a buyer purchase your home when he or she does not qualify for a full mortgage loan (*purchase money mortgage*)
□ paying a fee to the lender in order to reduce a buyer's monthly mortgage payments (*buying down a mortgage*)
□ paying part or all of a buyer's closing costs
□ paying the buyer's mortgage costs for a specified time period
□ covering maintenance costs for a specified time period
□ prepaying the buyer's taxes for a year
□ offering a gift of cash at closing to help buyers cover decorating or repair costs

Offering financing means that you may be able to sell your home faster and at a higher price. You also may able to claim some tax deductions. Whether you should do so or not depends on inter-est rates, the needs of the buyer, what you can afford, and the degree of risk with which you are comfortable. When interest rates are high or buyers have trouble qualifying for loans, the best route may be to help buyers reduce monthly mortgage costs. You can do that by buying down the interest rate on the buyer's mortgage, letting the buyer assume your assumable mortgage, or arranging a purchase money mortgage (see below).

For cash-strapped buyers who can handle monthly mortgage payments but lack substantial savings, consider covering closing costs, providing cash at the closing, or paying expenses or mortgage and maintenance payments during the early months. Many buyers have a difficult time coming up with the down payment; by helping pay their expenses you effectively put money back in their pockets. While reducing the price of your home will slightly lower buyers' mortgage payments and the agent's commission, it doesn't help buyers when they need money the most—usually at closing.

There are several serious drawbacks: Providing financing can cost you cash at the time of sale, create more work and worry for you, and—especially if you agree to take back a mortgage—cause you some financial risk. You don't have the resources of a bank to judge a buyer's credit-worthiness, so, before offering such financ-ing, get a real estate agent or your accountant to assess the buyer's financial situation. Also check with your accountant regarding your tax liability and the appropriate interest rate to charge the buyer. In addition, ask a real estate attorney to structure the transaction for your protection. Otherwise, problems might arise later that could lead to lawsuits and a foreclosure.

PURCHASE MONEY MORTGAGE

This is the most prevalent type of seller financing, especially when interest rates are high and buyers have a harder time qualifying for mortgages. If a buyer can't qualify for the full mortgage on your home through a lender, you can offer to "take back" a purchase money mortgage for the remaining amount. This means you hold a second mortgage for the buyer, who agrees to pay you principal and interest in monthly installments. (He or she sends a separate check to the primary lender.)

In any case, don't enter a purchase money mortgage arrangement lightly; it can be risky, especially because you are extending credit to a buyer unable to qualify for the full loan through a bank or some other lender. If you need all of the cash out of your home to buy another property, a purchase money mortgage is probably not for you.

Agreeing to a purchase money mortgage can also pose problems with lenders. Most lenders take the monthly payment owed the seller into consideration when deciding how much money to lend the buyer. That extra debt can further lower the amount the bank or mortgage company is willing to lend. The bigger the down payment the buyer contributes, the better, because that means the buyer has a greater stake in keeping up payments on the home. The bank then has a smaller and more secure debt on its books. Also, lenders look more favorably on a loan involving seller financing when the amount being financed by the seller is low. Consider the following two examples:

□ Bill and Barbara agree to buy your home for $180,000. They can afford $18,000 (10 percent) as a down payment. But because their income isn't high enough to allow them to qualify for the remaining $162,000 mortgage, the lender will give them only $150,000. To cover the shortfall of $12,000, you agree to hold a second mortgage for that amount.

□ David and Debbie agree to buy your home for $150,000. Their income qualifies them for a $120,000 mortgage, but they have only $10,000 for a down payment. You agree to lend them the extra $20,000 needed for a 20-percent down payment that allows them to qualify for an 80-percent mortgage.

Some lenders accept secondary financing if the buyers have an unblemished credit report and stable income; others do not, because they don't want buyers to have to pay another lender (you), which might cause them to default on their first mortgage. A lender who agrees to your providing financing for the buyer's down payment may raise the buyer's interest rate as compensation for the higher risk the lender assumes in providing such a mortgage.

A popular form of seller financing is the *balloon mortgage*, in which all or most interest is paid off during the term of the mortgage, and the entire principal is due at the end of the term. At that time the buyer may refinance the mortgage through a lender and, if home prices have been rising or interest rates dropping, he or she can pay off the balance owed you from equity in the home. Obviously, this is risky. If prices don't rise or interest rates don't go down, you may have to extend the loan.

The buyer may also owe a large portion of the principal when the loan comes due. Short-term mortgages are often structured to require monthly payments similar to those on a long-term (usually 30-year) mortgage. But since the purchase money mortgage comes due much sooner, and more interest than principal is paid during the early years, the buyer must pay a large lump sum of principal at the end of the loan period.

How to Structure the Loan

You and the buyer must negotiate the interest rate to be charged and the term of the loan, with the help of your agent and an attorney. Loan terms are generally for up to 10 years. You should charge the buyer an interest rate that is slightly above current levels. But when the market is down or interest rates are high, or if you are eager to sell, you might charge a 1- to 2-percent lower interest rate than other lenders. You can also take back a larger loan. Build in some protection against the risk you are taking as a below-market lender by setting your home's price a little higher, too.

Even in a more favorable market when interest rates are low, by charging 1 to 2 percent above the going interest rate, you can help a deal go through for buyers who can't quite qualify for full bank financing. In general, you should charge an even higher interest rate when you agree to a mortgage of more than five years. Ask your accountant to help determine the appropriate rate.

The reason to charge more is to compensate for the added risk you take. In either case, you benefit both by selling your property and by collecting a higher interest rate than your money is likely to earn elsewhere. You may even be able to sell the mortgage for cash to a mortgage broker or private investor, if the mortgage is structured correctly. You probably have to accept less than the loan's face value, however, because of the higher risk the investor is taking with your private loan.

Besides allowing buyers to purchase a home that would otherwise be out of their price range, a second mortgage provided by a seller can save the buyer money. The larger the loan you give the buyer, the less he or she has to pay in *points* to the commercial lender (points are fees charged by lenders at closing; each point equals 1 percent of the mortgage amount).

The buyer may also be able to avoid paying for *private mortgage insurance* (PMI) when the down payment is less than 20 percent, if you agree to lend the buyer whatever amount brings the down payment up to 20 percent. In a soft economy, lenders require PMI when buyers put only 5 to 10 percent down. The buyer pays for this insurance until the loan-to-value ratio on the home equals 80 percent or less. With only 5 percent down, for instance, the loan-to-value ratio starts out at 95 percent. Once a total of 20 percent of the principal has been paid off, or the home's value has risen sufficiently to bring the loan down to 80 percent or less of the market value, the buyer no longer has to pay for PMI.

Protecting Yourself Against Default

A qualified real estate attorney should draw up the contract for seller financing, and complete all the necessary paperwork. The attorney can also advise you on how to protect your interests should the buyer default on payments to you.

If one payment is late, act quickly. Immediately contact the buyer to find out why the check failed to arrive. Your contract with the buyer should have provided for a late penalty, plus provisions for the payment of legal fees and costs if it is necessary for you to take legal action.

If default occurs, you have several alternatives: (a) absorb the loss; (b) sue the buyer against his or her assets, income, or other property; or (c) start a foreclosure action. Usually, if the buyer defaults on your loan, he or she probably also defaulted on the loan from the primary lender. (Call the lender to find out if this is the case.)

Before you take legal action, contact the buyer for a reasonable explanation for the missing payment. Perhaps the buyer has been laid off, is ill, or has run up too many debts. Some problems can be worked out; others, such as long-term unemployment, will probably lead eventually to bankruptcy and foreclosure.

In times of rising home values, foreclosure is less of a concern, because it is likely that the first and second mortgage holders will get their money back on the home. During times of flat or declining home values, though, lenders are anxious to avoid foreclosures. They prefer to look for ways to work out the buyer's problems, such as extending the loan period or arranging credit counseling. If you and the buyer cannot work out a solution, or the buyer is uncooperative, contact the primary lender; perhaps the lender's influence and help can persuade the buyer to repay the loan. Or you can obtain additional collateral from the buyer as future security for the buyer's obligations.

If the bank does foreclose on the home, you will get paid only after the first mortgage holder—the savings-and-loan, bank, or mortgage company—receives its money in full. So if home prices have declined since the sale, you may not get paid at all.

To guard against this eventuality, take the following steps:

☐ Check your buyer's financial and employment history and credit record. Request a credit report from TRW or another national credit bureau. Your real estate agent may also ask the buyer to sign a consent form for the seller's attorney to request a credit report from TRW. Unless the buyer has a good explanation, be wary of a pattern of late payments on previous mortgages or other debts.

☐ Ask the buyer to fill out a credit application (available from a bank) that details income, assets, and debts. Look for a buyer who has a steady income, manageable debt, and some cash reserves. If the buyer's income is low now, does he or she have good prospects for the near future? Perhaps the buyer is a recent law or medical graduate who can expect high earnings in a few years, at least by the time a balloon payment is due.

☐ Ask the buyer for a copy of his or her most recent tax return.

☐ Request a minimum 10-percent down payment from the buyer, so that the buyer has a substantial sum to lose if he or she defaults. Of course, since purchase money mortgages are often used to help buyers who cannot afford large down payments, this condition may eliminate buyers who most need your financing. Weigh that possibility against your own financial risk.

☐ Ask the buyer to have someone else guarantee to repay the loan (a cosigner or guarantor) to you if he or she runs into financial trouble. Your lawyer should help you document this guarantee.

☐ If you are serving as a primary lender for the buyer (i.e., you are lending the buyer more than a bank), ask your lawyer to build in default clauses and spell out the conditions under which you can reclaim your property.

☐ Have your lawyer record the second mortgage with your county or the appropriate agency. This record will show you have a stake in the property should the buyer default. For the buyer, recording the mortgage serves as proof that your loan is a tax-deductible mortgage with interest payments that can be used as tax deductions.

☐ If you are providing all of the financing, you may want to require the buyer to pay any real estate taxes directly to you. You in turn make the payments to the tax authorities. This strategy protects you, the mortgage holder, in case the buyer fails to pay the taxes on his or her own.

ASSUMABLE MORTGAGES

A mortgage is *assumable* if it can be transferred to a buyer, often at the same interest rate. The buyer pays the seller the difference between the sales price and the amount remaining on the mortgage.

An assumable mortgage with a low interest rate is an important incentive to buyers when interest rates are high and it's difficult to obtain and afford a loan. Most fixed-rate loans made since 1980 are not assumable, however, except for those issued by the FHA and the VA. An adjustable-rate mortgage (ARM) is assumable sometimes. To find out if your mortgage is in this category, check with your lender.

The conditions under which your mortgage is assumable may vary, too. The lender has to approve the buyer's credit-worthiness and, depending on the terms of your original contract, may even be able to increase the interest rate. If your mortgage agreement contains a due-on-sale clause, your loan must be paid off at the time of the sale. In that case, you must get permission from the lender for the buyer to take over the loan.

There are other problems that limit the assumability of most mortgages. Since the majority of assumable mortgages were made years ago, the balances remaining on those mortgages are now relatively low. For a buyer today to assume such a mortgage, he or she has to have a large amount of cash to pay the difference between the mortgage and the current market value of the home. For example, if you bought your home for $100,000 in 1980 and took out an $80,000 mortgage for 30 years at 6 percent, in 1993 the loan balance would be about $60,000. If your selling price is $150,000, a buyer has to pay you $90,000 cash to assume your mortgage. So the value of old assumable mortgages is negligible to buyers who live in areas that have experienced high appreciation in home values.

FHA AND VA MORTGAGES

FHA mortgage loans are rarely provided for higher-priced homes because of the dollar limits on the mortgage amount. VA loans don't require any down payment by the buyer, and carry a low interest rate. They are available to veterans of the armed forces and are assumable by nonveterans as well. Like FHA loans, VA mortgages are guaranteed by the federal government.

FHA and VA mortgages are assumable as long as the lender approves the buyers—that is, finds them credit-worthy. The VA requires a processing funding fee for the assumption of a loan made after March 1, 1988.

Complex rules govern the assumption of FHA loans and any future liability to the seller. If you have an FHA loan, ask your broker or agent to explain the rules governing the assumption of such a loan.

BUY-DOWN MORTGAGES

A less risky but initially more expensive form of seller financing is for the seller to "buy down" a buyer's mortgage interest rate and thus reduce his or her payments. Typically, you pay a percentage (usually 1 to 3 percent) of the loan amount to the lender to reduce the buyer's interest rate. There are advantages to you, too. By offering lower interest rates that reduce monthly payments, you may avoid having to lower your price and may attract many more buyers. You can also deduct the cost of a buy-down from your home's cost basis as a selling expense to reduce capital gains (see chapter 2).

There are two types of buy-downs: *temporary* and *permanent*. Temporary buy-downs reduce the interest rate and mortgage pay-

HOW A BUY-DOWN MORTGAGE WORKS

On a $150,000 mortgage with a standard 2 to 1 buy-down of the interest rate, the seller pays the buyer's lender a portion of the monthly mortgage payment for two years. That payment cuts the buyer's interest rate by 2 percent for the first year of the loan and 1 percent for the second year, after which the interest reverts to the full rate.

So if the interest rate on the loan is 9 percent, the seller's share of the financing reduces it to 7 percent for the first year and 8 percent for the second. In the third year, and for the rest of the loan, it rises to the full rate of 9 percent.

Here's how such a buy-down affects the buyer's loan payments on a $150,000 mortgage at 9 percent for 30 years:

	9 Percent Monthly Payment		Buyer's Reduced Monthly Payment		Monthly Subsidy from Seller	Yearly Subsidy from Seller
Year 1	$1,206.94	−	$ 997.96	=	$208.98	$2,507.76
Year 2	$1,206.94	−	$1,100.65	=	$106.29	1,275.48
					Total	$3,783.24

So the total cost to the seller of making this buy-down is $3,783.24.

ments for a specified period, say two or three years. Permanent buy-downs last the life of the loan. One such buy-down has the seller paying an extra point, which reduces the interest rate by one-eighth for the life of the mortgage. For obvious reasons, most seller-financed residential buy-downs are temporary.

Taking back a second mortgage for a buyer sends up a red flag for many lenders, who often sell their loans to the secondary mortgage market and must meet strict standards. But almost all lenders accept buy-downs as long as certain guidelines are followed. These guidelines, set by the Federal National Mortgage Association (Fannie Mae), Federal Home Loan Mortgage Corporation (Freddie Mac), FHA, and VA, include limiting the annual increase on a temporary buy-down to 1 percent. That percentage represents the advantage of buy-downs to buyers over adjustable-rate mortgages, which may rise 2 percent a year. When the buyer puts down less than 10 percent on a conventional mortgage, you are limited by the rules to paying 3 percent of the sales price toward a buy-down. When the buyer puts down 10 percent or more on a conventional or FHA loan, you are limited to paying 6 percent of the sales price.

To buy down a mortgage by 1 percent *permanently*, you probably need to pay around five points (5 percent of the loan amount). The actual amount depends on how much of a down payment the buyer makes; the smaller the down payment, the greater the cost of the buy-down, since the loan amount is larger. For a short-term buy-down of 1 percent off the interest rate, you pay less—about 1 percent of the mortgage.

A $5,000 buy-down can be more effective than reducing the price of your home because it not only decreases your buyer's mortgage payments but also allows the buyer to qualify for a bigger loan. Most lenders will qualify buyers according to the newly reduced interest rate, and a lower rate means a buyer can afford more house.

The procedures for making the buy-down are simple. At the closing, you write a check to the lender for the total amount you are contributing; the money goes into an escrow account and is paid out of that account monthly to the lender.

OTHER BUYER SUBSIDIES

Another way to keep cash in a buyer's wallet and persuade a buyer to purchase your home over a similar one is for you to pay the closing costs, including title search, title insurance, legal fees, home inspection, and points. Making such concessions is equivalent to reducing the price, in tax terms: you can deduct the amount you pay from your capital gains tax. The buyer, however, loses the tax deductions available had the buyer paid those expenses. Lenders do limit the amount you can contribute, because Fannie Mae applies strict guidelines to the mortgages it purchases from lenders.

You might also offer to pay the buyer's mortgage (principal and interest) payments for a set period, say, for three to six months. On a $150,000 mortgage at 9 percent, your costs would be about $4,800. Again, that may be more useful to the buyer than a price reduction, especially if cash is tight.

Other options are to offer to pay the first year of taxes (also a tax-deductible expense), the homeowner's insurance, maintenance fees for a co-op or condo, or cash for decorating or repair work suggested by an inspection report or requested by the buyer. Anything that eases a buyer's financial burden during the first year of home ownership can make your home more attractive and affordable. Before you make any offers, though, check with your accountant on the tax implications for you and the buyer, and be sure the buyer is aware of any loss of tax deductions. If you're flexible on the kind of subsidy you're willing to provide, you greatly increase the odds of selling your home.

HELPING BUYERS FIND LOW-COST, CONVENTIONAL FINANCING

Even if you can't or aren't willing to finance a buyer's purchase, you (or your agent) can help a buyer locate a low-interest loan, or one with no points or low points. Tell the buyer to shop around for mortgage rates, since they can vary by as much as 1 percent from lender to lender. Suggest that the buyer contact HSH Associates in Butler, New Jersey (phone 800-873-2837) for their Homebuyer's Mortgage Kit. The kit contains a listing of interest rates for various types of mortgages, updated weekly, from local banks and mortgage companies in 30 states. Most major populated areas are covered. The kit also includes a 44-page booklet explaining types of mortgages, how to calculate effective interest rates, how to shop for title insurance, and other relevant topics.

Up-to-date mortgage information is also available on CNN's "MoneyWeek" program. Check local listings for the date and time.

If your buyer is a veteran, he or she should also look into applying for a Veterans Administration loan. These are usually low-cost, no-down-payment loans, although high loan amounts (currently above $144,000) require a down payment. The seller must pay the points for a VA loan.

For buyers who meet maximum income and mortgage guidelines, a Federal Housing Administration loan may be appropriate. FHA loans require small down payments (5 percent of the home's appraised value) and charge interest rates slightly below current rates for conventional loans. They involve some additional costs as well, which change from time to time. A real estate agent or lender can provide information about exact fees and rules and determine whether a buyer qualifies.

Some states also have programs to help first time home buyers or low-income home buyers. Often these mortgages carry a below-market interest rate. To find out about these state-assisted mortgages, have your buyer contact his or her state government office.

10

Selling a Condo or a Co-op

Most of the information in this book applies to co-ops and condos as well as to single-family dwellings. But selling a co-op or condo entails some extra considerations that sellers of detached single-family homes do not face. This chapter gives an overview of some of the extra challenges of selling your co-op or condo, along with some marketing strategies.

WHAT IS A CONDO?

A *condominium*, or "condo," is a building with multiple housing units; each resident owns outright his or her individual unit. The common areas of the complex, such as the lobby, courtyard, basement, and land, are owned jointly by all the owners of the units.

All condo owners automatically become members of the condominium association, a group that collectively controls and manages the complex. Major decisions are made by the condo board, a panel of representative owners selected by the association members. While the condo board makes the decisions, the day-to-day management and administration of the condo are most often handled by an outside real estate management company hired by the board.

WHAT IS A CO-OP?

A *cooperative apartment*, also called a stock cooperative or co-op, is also a building or complex with multiple units, with the difference that tenants do not actually own the apartments or units they live in. Rather, they own stock in the corporation that owns the building or complex. Purchase of that stock includes a proprietary lease giving a tenant the right to occupy a particular unit. In other words, the apartment (or other type of unit, such as a town house) is owned, as is the entire building and the land, by the corporation, and the tenants are all shareholders of the owner corporation.

This technical distinction results in one substantial difference for you as the seller: Because there is no individual ownership of the units in a co-op, it can be somewhat more difficult for buyers to obtain a mortgage to purchase your co-op than to secure a mortgage to buy a condo or single-family house.

FINDING A CONDO OR CO-OP BROKER

While some real estate agents are generalists who sell every type of residential housing, others cater to a particular trade. If you can, find a broker or agent who specializes in co-op or condo sales, or at least try to hire one who has had experience with buyers looking for co-op or condo living. You can do this in several ways:

Ask Other Residents. Are there other owners in your apartment complex or town house development who are selling—or have recently sold—their units? Ask them for the names of their real estate brokers. Inquire if they were satisfied with the agent's or broker's services, how quickly the unit sold, and how their sale price compared with their original listing or asking price.

Check Nearby Buildings or Developments. Drive by buildings or complexes near you that are of similar quality. If you see any For Sale signs, jot down the phone numbers, then call the brokers. Explain that you have a co-op or condo for sale, then follow the guidelines in chapter 7 for selecting and working with a broker or agent.

Check Co-op/Condo For Sale Ads. Check the local newspapers or free real estate "magazines" distributed in supermarkets. If they contain many ads offering co-ops and condos for sale, ask the agents and brokers representing these properties to help you.

If you prefer to sell on your own, follow the guidelines in chapter 6. Check your co-op bylaws or condo deed to see if there are any restrictions on selling activities. For example, some co-op complexes do not allow For Sale signs to be placed in front of the building or a unit.

THE PROSPECTIVE BUYER

Co-ops and condos are typically bought by young singles, newlyweds, retirees, empty-nesters, divorced or widowed people, and buyers in middle and lower income brackets. The condo market is less attractive to families with children, who prefer detached homes with private yards.

At the high end of the co-op/condo market are the luxury town houses selling for $200,000 to $300,000 and up. Many young, high-income couples find the luxury condo a nice intermediate housing alternative, giving them the peace and quiet of the suburbs, without the hassle of home maintenance and upkeep, in a luxury setting.

The primary appeal of a condo or co-op is that it costs less than a detached home. The negative aspect of buying a condo or co-op is that its value doesn't increase as much as a house in the same area, so you may get less when you sell.

Buyers are often confused about whether they should purchase a condo or a co-op. Condos are often more desirable because financing and reselling a condo are easier; lenders are also more willing to finance the purchase of a condo than a co-op. And condos do not usually require the approval of a buyer by a board of directors, as do co-ops. On the other hand, co-ops are attractive to buyers who prefer a greater degree of compatibility with their neighbors and welcome stricter controls over subletting and selling of units.

Buyers for your unit, whether condo or co-op, will also want to know about *maintenance fees, reserve funds, subletting practices,* and *other important financial considerations.*

Maintenance Fees

When you buy a single-family home, your fixed monthly expenses include the mortgage and property tax payments. Maintenance of the home is a nonfixed cost—you might have no significant repair costs for two years, then need to spend $4,000 almost immediately to replace a leaky roof.

In a co-op or condo, owners are charged a set monthly maintenance fee that can be raised periodically to cover repair costs, escalating expenses for the building, or other special needs. The fee is set by a vote of the board of directors within the guidelines set forth in the co-op or condo bylaws.

Items typically covered by the maintenance fee include doorman service, cable TV, parking, laundry room, exterminating service, central air-conditioning, closed-circuit security, sports and recreational facilities, outdoor lighting, lawn care, pool service, exterior maintenance, water, sewers, and trash removal. The monthly fee also includes your share of any underlying mortgage costs, taxes, and insurance.

First-time buyers often view the maintenance fee as the most negative aspect of co-op or condo living. Their perception is based on the erroneous view that there are no maintenance costs associated with single-home ownership. In fact, the cost of home repairs and maintenance for a house can be astronomical. If you average out your maintenance expenditures by the number of months you live in the house, they are often greater than the maintenance fee for a co-op of comparable size and quality.

Don't hesitate to point this out to buyers who object to the maintenance fee. Remind them that although $600 a month may seem high, they'll never have to spend $7,500 for new aluminum siding, $2,500 for a new furnace, $3,000 for roof repairs, or $6,500 to replace the plumbing. Of course, maintenance costs also can increase in order to cover large expenditures by the condo or co-op. There is always the possibility of an *assessment* (a one-time payment levied on all the tenants) to pay for new plumbing or roof repair, for example. But there is some comfort in the fact that the costs are shared by all the unit owners and the burden of accepting bids and supervising the work is done by an experienced building manager.

Reserve Funds

A reserve fund is an amount of money set aside by the co-op or condo corporation to pay for capital improvements, routine maintenance, unexpected repairs, and other expenses that come up from time to time.

If your management has an adequate or more than adequate reserve fund, that's a selling point to stress to buyers. A substantial reserve fund ensures that unexpected repairs and expenses can be paid for with cash on hand.

Without enough ready funds to cover a repair or improvement, the corporation either has to do without the improvement, delay the repair, increase the maintenance fees to raise funds for the work, or levy an assessment on each unit owner. For this reason, many buyers are reluctant to buy into a building with low reserves.

Subletting

Buyers who are considering the purchase of your unit as an investment or as a vacation home want to be able to rent the unit when they are not occupying it.

In most condos, owners have almost unlimited freedom to rent to the tenant they want at whatever price the market will bear. In a co-op, however, the bylaws may dictate whether buyers can sublet their units.

If there's no rule about subletting one way or the other, then the buyer is probably free to sublet. However, the lack of a specific subletting clause means the board can vote at any time to *ban* subletting, without the vote being subject to approval by the shareholders. Be prepared also to share a percentage of your rent receipts with the co-op corporation. In times of economic hardship or when sales are sluggish, co-op boards frequently allow owners to rent their units for a period of two years, although they reserve the right to screen all rental applicants.

If the right to sublet is granted to original buyers in a new co-op or co-op conversion, and this right is spelled out in the prospectus and bylaws, the board cannot arbitrarily decide to suspend the subletting privilege.

Other Important Financial Considerations

Buyers are also concerned with such issues as the size of the underlying co-op mortgage (if there is one), the condition of the building, and the owner-occupancy rate.

A large mortgage balance on the building may mean the co-op corporation will have trouble borrowing money in the future to pay for the cost of repairs or upkeep that the reserve fund does not cover; lenders do not give large loans to associations that already service a substantial monthly debt.

Major structural or maintenance problems, especially those that are not immediately obvious, must be revealed to the buyer. Sellers and agents are increasingly obliged to disclose fully all defects and problems; failure to do so prior to sale could result in a lawsuit later on. Also, the American Institute of Certified Public Accountants now requires that CPAs handling a cooperative's books include on their annual audit statements an estimate of anticipated future repair and replacement costs for the building.

Finally, be prepared to tell buyers how many of the units have been sold and are currently occupied by the owners. In a *co-op conversion* (when a rental building converts to co-op ownership), the co-op corporation may be unable to get a bank loan to make needed repairs or improvements if a large number of units remain unsold. The existence of a large number of unsold units also reduces the value of your apartment.

CO-OP BOARDS

As stated previously, condo owners own their individual units and have the same clear title of ownership as the owner of a detached home.

Co-op owners, however, own shares in the co-op corporation that in turn owns the building. With those shares is included a proprietary lease on the owner's individual unit. When you sell, you transfer ownership by selling your shares of stock to your buyer; that ownership transfer includes the proprietary lease.

Usually the transfer of shares is not direct from seller to buyer. The seller turns in his or her shares to the co-op management or board, which then issues new shares in the name of the new buyer. In any event, the co-op board of directors has control over the sale; the degree of control is dictated by the terms of your co-op agreement.

As a rule, this control is fairly strong. The board is usually vested with the authority to screen potential residents, and usually can accept or reject prospective buyers at its sole discretion, without stating any reasons for its decision. The purpose is not to make your life difficult but to assure all the unit owners that only desirable and financially stable tenants are allowed to buy into the building.

THE CONDO OR CO-OP
HOME OFFICE

As a rule, a condo or co-op buyer can work from home if the business does not require any of the following:

- ☐ visits from customers or clients
- ☐ storage of inventory or materials
- ☐ frequent deliveries or other activities necessitating high volumes of commercial traffic
- ☐ selling of goods on the premises
- ☐ anything that detracts from the outside appearance of the unit (e.g., no commercial signs)
- ☐ activities or processes that create excessive noise

Your buyer could work from home as a consultant, writer, artist, computer programmer, or at some other pursuit that's fairly solitary and involves mostly desk work. The buyer can also work as a mason, carpenter, painter, contractor, plumber, electrician, or in similar occupations, provided he or she does not park a truck or van in the driveway or in front of a residential unit.

If you have a spare bedroom or a room designated as a home office, that's a selling point. First, though, you should make sure it can legally be used as such. Visit your town's municipal building and check the zoning regulations for your street to see what type of home-based business activities (if any) are allowed.

The law theoretically prevents discrimination based on race, religion, national origin, or ethnic background. Rejection of a buyer by a board may be based on income, financial status, or occupation, because the possibility of a buyer's failure to keep up with monthly maintenance payments harms the entire co-op. However, many people feel that some co-op boards wield their discriminatory power arbitrarily and reject certain potential buyers based on race, personality, or religious or sexual preference. Regardless of whether or not that's true, a board of directors can legally and at its discretion approve or disapprove any buyer.

Check your co-op agreement to see what restrictions apply to your buyers. Obviously, you will sell faster by accepting offers only from a buyer you feel is likely to be accepted by the board.

Also, don't alienate the board if you can help it. Be polite and agreeable rather than angry and argumentative, especially if they actually reject one of your buyers. Most boards want to have salable units, and a rejection is almost always based on financial considerations.

CONDO BOARDS

Condo boards generally have far less control over who buys into the building than do co-op boards, and they usually do not screen buyers.

Some condo boards retain a *right of first refusal*, which means the board is given the right to buy your unit at the same price your buyer offers you. If the condo board doesn't match your price or exercise its right of first refusal, then you're free to offer your unit for sale, unrestricted, on the open market, with no further approvals or interference.

Each condominium association operates under a set of written bylaws that govern the management and daily operations of the complex. These bylaws are in the papers given to you when you purchased your unit; if you can't find them, ask your condo board for a copy. Having these bylaws handy enables you to answer buyers' questions concerning the rules and regulations of your development.

FINANCING A CONDO OR CO-OP

Most of the information given previously on mortgage and financing procedures for houses applies equally to condos and co-ops. However, you should be aware of a few additional financing facts.

The first concerns the ability of your potential buyer to obtain financing. The rule of thumb is that mortgage payments, including principal, interest, taxes, and insurance, should amount to no more than about one-quarter of the buyer's gross monthly income for that buyer to qualify for a mortgage.

For a co-op or condo, the maintenance fee is included in this figure. Therefore, a buyer earning $6,000 a month qualifies for a mortgage on a house that carries a monthly mortgage payment of $1,500. But a buyer does *not* qualify for a mortgage on a co-op for the same amount of money, because the monthly mortgage payment of $1,500 *plus* the maintenance fee ($100 or more per month) will exceed one-quarter of his or her gross income.

These figures are not exact; in some cases the monthly payments of the mortgage holder can be as high as 28 to 36 percent of gross income. The point is that you must include maintenance fees when evaluating whether a buyer will be able to obtain financing for your unit.

Another point, already mentioned, is that banks as a rule are more willing to give loans for the purchase of a condo or a single-family home than for a co-op, because co-op ownership entails shares in a corporation rather than a piece of real estate. When a bank forecloses on a condo or detached house, it gets real property; when the same bank forecloses on a cooperative apartment, it receives only shares in the co-op corporation and rights under the proprietary lease.

Aside from the mortgage each individual unit owner holds on his or her shares, the cooperative corporation holds an underlying mortgage on the entire property. Because the corporation has a large mortgage payment to make each month, the amount of personal financing allowed may be limited, so the buyer may have to come up with a larger down payment than is normally required when buying a condo or house.

In addition to the cost of the unit, the size of the mortgage, the monthly maintenance fee, and the buyer's gross income, the buyer's ability to get financing also depends on the lending institution.

Some local lenders are more willing to make co-op loans than others, and a knowledgeable real estate agent can match the buyer with a source of financing. There usually isn't a problem if at least half the units in the cooperative are sold, and the sponsor is not in default or behind on mortgage payments.

The type and location of units is also important. Lenders may be hesitant to make loans on studios and one-bedroom apartments, on units in small buildings, and on upper-floor walkups. These less desirable apartments are difficult for the bank to resell on the open market, should the mortgage holder default. If you want to sell a small unit, try to locate and identify in advance one or two financial institutions you are reasonably sure will seriously consider your buyer's loan application.

Even when financing can be obtained, many banks and mortgage companies penalize co-op buyers by charging an interest rate that is .5 percent or 1 percent higher than for a condo or house. Some also require larger down payments for co-op purchases.

Finally, as in any home-selling situation, owner financing can help make the deal affordable and close the sale for you. Some incentives worth considering are (a) leasing the unit with an option to buy at a fixed purchase price, (b) offering to take back a second mortgage, (c) offering to pay the first year's maintenance fees, (d) offering to pay any increase in maintenance fees for the first three years, and (e) offering to pay closing costs.

11

Choosing an Alternative Selling Strategy

If the more conventional means of selling your home haven't worked, you still have a few alternatives. They may not be your first choice, and may even be a last resort, but these methods can lead to financial relief and an eventual sale.

AUCTIONS

Auctions of residential real estate have become increasingly commonplace in the last few years. According to the National Association of Realtors, 19,175 single-family homes (out of a total of 3.2 million) and 20,523 condos and co-ops (out of a total of 359,000) were sold at auction in the first half of 1991.

Auctions work well for selling residences, but not necessarily at market prices. In the past, auctions were typically used as a sales method of last resort for a home that had not sold after many months on the market, usually for those sellers who had moved out and couldn't afford to continue paying the carrying costs of the home. (Each month that a home doesn't sell, interest and other carrying costs reduce the potential return on investment by about 2 percent.)

Today more home sellers are choosing to sell their homes at auction immediately, instead of waiting until the more conventional routes have failed. Many auctioneers claim that first putting a house or condo up for sale at auction makes sense. The home hasn't grown stale after months on the market, for example. In addition, the home's price hasn't been adversely affected by numerous price reductions.

Auction Pricing Procedures

The actual price received at auction depends on the market, on how successfully the auction house promotes the event, on the style of the auctioneer, on the type of buyers present, and on the type of auction.

The auction may be a *public* auction or a *sealed-bid* auction. At public auctions, buyers assemble at a specified time and place to compete openly against one another for one or more properties. With a sealed-bid auction, buyers get just one chance to submit a bid by a specified date and may never know the ultimate winning bid. The sealed-bid process often limits the price the seller receives, too, since the buyer submits the highest bid he or she *thinks* will get the property, not the highest price he or she is finally willing to pay. Understandably, then, public auctions are far more popular.

There are three types of pricing auctions to choose from, but not all are available in all parts of the country:

Absolute Auction.   Here the property is sold to the highest bidder. This procedure usually results in the highest bids, because buyers are eager for a bargain, and more attend this type of auction. The competitive nature of such an auction and the excitement generated by the auctioneer and a sizable crowd can help raise the winning bid to a higher figure than the seller initially thought possible.

Minimum-Bid Auction.   (Also called absolute-with-minimum-bid auction.) The property is not sold in this type of auction unless the highest bid is above a set minimum price. If the minimum price is low enough to arouse interest and to convince buyers they may save more money than in a conventional bidding process, this type of auction can be most effective in generating sales.

Auction with Reserve. You reserve the right to reject the highest bid in this type of auction. You may set this reserve price with the auction house so it is not known to the bidders. Since this arrangement favors the seller, not the buyer, it is the least attractive to prospects and may draw the fewest buyers. The high bidder must be told of your acceptance or rejection of the bid within 48 hours.

Usually, properties are sold at auction "as is," and buyers bid on a standard contract provided by the seller. Although some auctions allow the winning bidder to inspect a property after the auction, and even insert a clause that cancels the deal if the inspection report is bad, buyers typically must inspect the property before the auction. They also must have financing arranged (although some auction houses help with that aspect) and be preapproved by a lender for a maximum mortgage amount. Sellers of homes at auction do not provide financing; homes are on a cash sale basis. This simplifies the selling process and ensures that the deal goes quickly to closing.

When buyers inspect the residence, they are given legal documents on the property to review, including the title report and a copy of the sales contract. For condominiums, condo fees are stated and a copy of the public offering statement made available.

Bidders at the auction must usually bring a personal or cashier's check for a set amount determined in advance by the auctioneer. The amount varies from state to state and depending on the type of auction and property; in a minimum-bid auction, the bidder might be required to bring a check for 5 percent of the minimum bid. The winning bidder must usually also submit a check for 5 to 20 percent of the bid as a nonrefundable earnest money deposit. (However, if the property turns out not to have clear title—for example, if there is a lien against it by a contractor—the auction house refunds the deposit.)

The auction house specifies what type and amount of payment is expected of the winning bidder. In many states, consumer protection laws give buyers the right to back out of a real estate sale within a specified number of days.

Other Fees

Auctioneers typically charge 10 percent of the home's final sale price, but rates are negotiable. If the auctioneer can sell and market your home with a group of similar properties at the same time, rates should be lower.

In some parts of the country, the auctioneer's fee is paid by the buyer, not the seller, and is called a buyer's premium; in this arrangement the auctioneer adds his or her commission to the winning bid. In other areas, sellers add a 2- or 3-percent buyer's fee to the sale price to help cover the auctioneer's fee.

If a real estate broker or agent brings a buyer for your property to the auction and the deal closes, the auction house will pay the broker a negotiable commission, such as 3 percent. The broker or agent must register the client with the auction house before the sale, typically by a letter signed by both prospective buyer and agent. Some auction houses also pay a commission to brokers and agents who refer sellers to them.

Auctions may be conducted singly on site or in a ballroom-type setting en masse. The seller pays advertising costs, which typically run 1 to 3 percent of the value of the property. These costs may be included in the commission.

Choosing an Auctioneer

Most states require auctioneers to be bonded and have a license to sell real estate at auction. Look for auctioneers who are members of the National Auctioneers Association (NAA), a professional trade association that sets ethical standards for auctioneers. About 20 percent of NAA members take advanced training to join the Certified Auctioneers Institute (CAI). To find out if your state requires auctioneers to be licensed, write to CAI at 8880 Ballentine, Overland Park, KS 66214 (fax 913-894-5281). You can also order a free directory of qualified auctioneers through CAI.

Here are some other guidelines for choosing an auctioneer:

☐ Choose an auction house that specializes in or at least handles the type of property (condo, co-op, estate, or single-family home) you are selling.

☐ Make sure the auctioneer is handling the local, regional, or national advertising your property requires. Most homes are sold through local advertising, but multimillion-dollar estates or commercial or investment properties might require national mailing lists and media placement.

☐ Read the firm's brochure and note how professionally it is written, photographed, and printed. Does the brochure answer all of your questions? If not, is it easy to get the answers by calling the company?

☐ Attend several auctions in your area. Note whether the registration process is well organized and how well the staff puts buyers at ease and keeps the mood upbeat; also observe the size of the crowds and the style of the auctioneer. A member of the staff should explain and demonstrate the procedures before the auction begins and answer all questions cheerfully. Information about the properties to be auctioned should be presented clearly and thoroughly before the bidding starts.

☐ Get the names of the firm's last five or ten clients and call them. Find out how satisfied they were with the auctioneer's advertising and performance, and the prices their homes brought. Were the prices within the ranges the auctioneer predicted? If the homes were appraised, how close were the prices to the appraised values? (Homes sold at auction are not routinely appraised, rather the auction house tells you the price range for the winning bid.)

☐ Get bids from prospective auction houses and compare costs and services.

☐ Ask each auctioneer the price range in which he or she thinks your home will sell, and whether he or she will conduct the type of auction you want (absolute, minimum-bid, or auction with reserve).

☐ Ask the auctioneer whether your home should be marketed on site or in a group with other homes, and why. To be marketed successfully on site, a home should have curb appeal, be in good condition, and have plenty of on-site or on-street parking. Homes that are part of a development or in a condo or co-op complex are usually marketed on site as well, since buyers can view the different properties at will. Most important, a larger crowd is drawn to an on-site auction with a large number and variety of units to choose from.

☐ Find out how long the auctioneer has been auctioning real estate, how well the properties sold, and at what price.

RENTING

You can always lease your home to a tenant if you can't find a buyer. In a soft housing market, rentals tend to pick up, since people are reluctant or can't afford to buy. Talk to an agent who specializes in rentals to find out how much rent you can reasonably expect to receive for your home. If it covers your monthly mortgage payments, taxes, and insurance, that's a good start. But also consider the costs of repairs and maintenance, especially if you will be living too far away to oversee the property yourself. The tenant should pay for the utilities and heat, or you'll have to add those costs to your monthly expenses.

In addition, screen your tenant carefully to make sure you are getting someone with a good financial record. You or your agent should run an employment check to verify income and job stability, and a credit check to determine whether the prospective tenant has had any problems paying bills. Carefully check referrals from past landlords to make sure you end up with a tenant who will maintain your home. A tenant who damages or neglects your property, or fails to cooperate with agents, may make finding a buyer more difficult later on.

When problems do arise with a tenant, be professional, calm, and flexible. If you feel you don't have the time or the temperament to handle tenants' demands or crises, hire a professional manager for the property, and factor in that cost to your rental expenses.

You may be able to charge a higher rent if you agree to a month-to-month rental instead of requiring a yearly lease. Many transferred executives, college students, and young people often change jobs and living situations and desire that kind of flexibility. The market for monthly rentals in your area depends on whether there are large companies transferring or hiring new employees, a large college with many students seeking off-campus housing, or a resort or seasonal attraction that brings in many visitors looking for short-term accommodations. Of course, short-term rentals may result in more wear and tear on your property, so be sure to ask tenants for a security deposit.

The advantages of renting your home are that it stays occupied and is a deterrent to vandals, that you earn some income to cover your home's carrying costs, and that you can qualify for tax deductions on maintenance costs, taxes, insurance, depreciation, and losses.

Tax Consequences of Renting

Assuming you find a reliable tenant, the biggest disadvantage of renting is that you could lose your capital gains rollover benefit (see chapter 2). This could happen if you rent for an extended period, buy a more expensive replacement property (or one equal in price), or fail to sell your home within two years. If the IRS interprets the renting of your home as a conversion into a rental property, your home is disqualified as a primary residence for purposes of the rollover provision. The length of the rental and how actively you tried to sell the home during the rental period are just two factors that determine whether the property is considered a rental by the

IRS. Check with your accountant or a tax attorney before you proceed with renting, to determine both the tax consequences and whether renting makes financial sense for you.

LEASE WITH OPTION TO BUY

Under this arrangement, a potential buyer rents and maintains your home for a length of time, usually one to two years. At the end of that period, the tenant can decide to buy your home for a set price, which is determined before the tenant moves in. During the rental period, the tenant pays several hundred dollars more than a normal market rent each month; part of the rent—or sometimes all—is put aside for the down payment. Typically, however, 20 to 50 percent of the rent is applied toward the future down payment.

The agreement can also require the tenant to make an up-front payment of 3 to 5 percent of the home's price. Or, if none of the rent is to be applied to the down payment, the buyer can be asked instead to put down a nonrefundable deposit equal to 5 to 10 percent of the purchase price.

An option to buy is a good way to help buyers afford a home when interest rates and prices are high and when buyers don't have enough cash for a down payment. Other reasons to enter into such an arrangement are that you may need to move and don't want to leave your home unoccupied, or that you may want to delay paying capital gains taxes.

As stated previously, at the end of the predetermined period, the tenant has the option to purchase the property. You, on the other hand, are locked into the contract and must sell to the tenant if he or she decides to buy. The part of the monthly rent that was set aside becomes part of the down payment, and the tenant then pays you any remaining portion of the down payment due, and applies to a lender for a mortgage on the balance. If the tenant decides not to buy, he or she loses that portion of the reserved rent to you for having effectively taken the property off the market during the rental period.

Setting the Price

In a rising market, you have two choices when setting the price of your home at the time of the lease-option contract. You can either figure in the likely appreciation to your home's current fair market value in order to increase your profit, or let the tenant benefit from the projected equity as an incentive to go ahead with the purchase.

If home prices in your area are not appreciating, you can either set the price at your home's current market value (if prices appear to be relatively stable), or reduce the price according to an appraiser's estimate of how much prices will fall over the lease period. The latter is obviously risky, because markets can change. But if you're anxious to sell, agreeing to a lower set price motivates the tenant to buy. If you don't agree to factor in depreciation, you may not be able to find a tenant willing to go ahead with the lease option. A third possibility is to renegotiate the price and term when the option expires.

Advantages and Disadvantages

There are several advantages to the seller in a lease option, especially in a slow market.

If the tenant doesn't purchase at the end of the rental period, you will have still collected an above-market rent. You are also able to claim tax deductions and depreciation based on income tax laws applicable to rental property.

An option to buy increases the chances of making a sale because it opens up the possibility of home ownership to a bigger pool of prospects—people who might not be able to afford a home any other way. An option arrangement also encourages tenants to save money via a forced-payment plan so they can buy your home.

Finally, your home will be occupied and presumably well taken care of in your absence.

The disadvantages of a lease option are fairly obvious. The tenant may decide not to purchase at the end of the term and you have to start over again finding a buyer or a new tenant. Or, worse, the tenant may later discover he or she still can't afford to buy your home and perhaps fail to keep it up. Depending on the contract, your home may also have been off the market for that time and you may have lost opportunities to sell to more qualified buyers. In the worst-case scenario, the tenant may discontinue payments partway through the agreed-on rental period and you may have to start eviction proceedings.

Consult an Attorney

The terms and conditions of lease options are flexible and variable. Check with a lawyer to be sure the contract cannot be construed as an installment land contract or a delayed sale by the IRS—for example, if the rent paid is unusually high and most or all of the rent is applied toward the down payment. If the buyer will obviously suffer a large financial loss by not exercising the option, the agreement may be considered a sale from the start.

Lease-with-option-to-buy contracts have many possible variations that depend on any number of factors; an experienced real estate attorney can help work out the terms of your agreement according to your needs and those of the prospective buyer. The goal is to make the agreement fair to both parties, so that a deal favorable to both can eventually take place.

RIGHT OF FIRST REFUSAL

Another type of lease that can be granted separately or combined with a lease option gives a tenant the first chance to buy your home when the property is offered for sale. This kind of agreement is usually made when finding a renter is difficult and there is pressure from the prospective tenant to grant a right of first refusal. Obviously, it makes selling your home more difficult. If you do receive an offer from a buyer, you must first check with the tenant, who has the right of first refusal, before you can accept. Depending on the length of time specified by your contract with the tenant, the buyer who made the offer may get discouraged and go elsewhere.

The right of first refusal usually gives the tenant the option to buy your home at the same price and terms as were offered by the other buyer. Always seek a lawyer's advice before drawing up such an agreement.

HOUSE-SWAPPING

The least common way to "sell" a home is swapping or trading residences. Nevertheless, this practice has gained some popularity, especially in poor markets. The advantage of swapping is that it eliminates the need to find a first-time buyer, as in conventional home selling.

Here's how a swap works: You negotiate trading homes with another seller who is looking for a home similar to yours. One party may be trading up and the other down, or both parties may be making a fairly even trade, but each wants to move into a different area. The types of homes traded can be very different, even if the cost is similar. For example, the owner of a suburban executive home may wish to trade with the owner of an urban condo or co-op. Whoever moves into the more expensive home has, in effect, given his or her home as a down payment, and must pay the cash difference to the trade-down seller. Of course, both homes may have nonassumable mortgages that must be paid off, so each buyer will have to obtain a new mortgage. This would not be the case in the situation of an older seller, with no mortgage, who is trading down.

Instead of a deal involving three parties—the buyer of your home, you, and the seller of the home you want to move into—there are just two parties. So you eliminate one set of problems and contingencies. Another advantage is that setting a possession date for both homes is straightforward: owners switch on an agreed-on day, with no need to move into temporary quarters.

The difficulty with house-swapping is that the chances of two sellers wanting to trade homes with each other are fairly low. Unless you can find an agency or broker who has a data base of other sellers who want to trade, you are limited in your choices. This may change if house-swapping continues to become more popular and brokers take an active role in promoting and facilitating the exchange of properties.

12

Negotiating the Price with Your Buyer

□

The first principle of negotiating price with buyers is that smart marketing done early on puts you in a stronger negotiating position later. The more aggressively you market and advertise your home, the more buyers you attract. The more buyers you attract, the more offers you get.

When you have offers from more than one buyer, you are obviously ahead, because the buyers are then competing with one another to get your house. When you have only one potential buyer, he or she is competing only with you, not with other buyers.

You always do better when the buyer wants your home more than you necessarily want to sell it to that particular buyer. The easiest way to put yourself in that position is to have offers from multiple buyers.

IMPROVING YOUR NEGOTIATING POWER

There are various strategies that can help put you in a superior position as you enter into negotiations with a buyer.

Find a Motivated Buyer

If you can find a buyer who has to buy, and soon, you may get a better price. Such a buyer is often less concerned with price than with closing the deal, and this makes him or her easier to work with in negotiations.

How do you find a motivated buyer? Listen for clues. If a buyer casually mentions that he or she has already sold the condo and must move by the first of next month, you know you have a needy buyer. If a buyer says that the search has been going on for a long time, that, too, may indicate a strong desire to find a home.

Corporate transfers can also produce motivated buyers. Moving to a new job in a new state is pressure enough without the added headache of living in a motel and spending weekends house-hunting. In addition, corporate executives who receive generous relocation aid are often not as price-sensitive as locals.

Know Your Buyer

Although well-off people are as bargain-conscious as most families on a budget, the wealthier prospect has the money to meet your demands if he or she *really* wants your home.

Have your broker or agent ask buyers how much money they have for a down payment and whether they are qualified to get a mortgage for the balance. Most experienced agents determine how much house buyers can afford even before showing them properties. If you are selling on your own, ask the same question of interested buyers; they will expect you to make this inquiry, and it will save both you and the buyers a lot of time and wasted effort.

Where buyers are moving from and to is another indicator. Prospects moving from the city to the suburbs are usually less price-conscious than buyers already living in the suburbs. That's because suburban buyers are typically moving up from a starter house to a larger home. They are using most of their available cash, so asking for an extra $5,000 can make them walk away from a deal. The same is usually true of first-time buyers, who lack the equity of move-up buyers. On the other hand, city dwellers are often going from an expensive small apartment to a bigger home that is costing them less than the equivalent apartment. As a result, they are already pleased with the "bargain" they feel they are getting, and won't be fazed by having to pay a few thousand dollars more. This is not a hard-and-fast rule, though.

Sell Your Old House First

Start house-hunting after you put your home on the market, if you like, but delay signing a contract for a new property until after you've closed on your old home.

If you have to close on your new home before you have sold the old property, you will be carrying two mortgages, plus other expenses. This outlay can quickly drain your cash reserves, and the financial pressure of keeping up huge monthly payments will turn you into a motivated seller if not a desperate one, eager to accept any offer that comes along.

What if you find your dream house? You may feel compelled to buy it, but at least try to get a clause in the contract that makes final sale of the new property contingent on your selling your existing home. Few sellers will grant this contingency, however.

Don't Vacate Your Home

Even if you already own another home, don't move out of your current home until it is sold. An empty house is much harder to sell. Market studies have shown that a house can command a selling price 10 to 15 percent higher when it's furnished and occupied.

Furthermore, an unoccupied home is a signal to buyers that you have probably bought a new residence and are under financial pressure to sell quickly. Buyers become less inclined to raise their offer in that case.

If you absolutely must move, arrange for a tenant or house-sitter to take your place (see chapter 8).

Don't Set a Deadline for Moving

Try not to put yourself in the position where you have to move or sell by a certain date. If you have made arrangements to move to another area in a short time, and your home is not sold, don't panic. Rent an apartment in the new area and have a spouse, relative, or friend occupy your old home until it is sold. Obviously, having to sell by a certain date puts you at a serious disadvantage when negotiating a sale.

Keep Your Finances to Yourself

Most buyers realize that if you bought your home many years ago, when prices were substantially lower, you will earn a large profit on the sale even if you sell below your asking price. As a result, they'll push for a lower price.

Refrain from telling buyers the amount of your mortgage balance or the total amount of debt (mortgage and home equity loans) secured by the property. Buyers who know you have little debt left on the house may assume that your price is negotiable indeed.

Although buyers can find out from real estate agents how long your home has been on the market, don't tell them if they don't ask. They'll assume you're anxious and willing to negotiate if the home has been listed for some time.

THE BROKER OR AGENT'S ROLE

Your broker or agent can be a valuable aid during the negotiating period. He or she should act as a go-between and communicate offers and counteroffers between you and the buyer. An agent should help you get the most reasonable price possible for your home, and give you a realistic assessment of how high he or she thinks the buyer will go.

As stated previously, the agent is working for you, the seller;

you are paying the broker and agent a fee in exchange for helping you sell your home at the highest price you can get.

In that capacity, he or she should give you an accurate assessment of the buyer's mood and intentions, along with advice on what to counteroffer and how to respond in negotiations.

At the same time, acting as your agent, the real estate professional ideally should keep confidential any information you may reveal. For example, if you tell your agent the rock-bottom price at which you're willing to sell, the agent should not divulge this information to the buyer. In the real world, however, the agent is working to get a deal that is good for all three parties: the seller, the buyer, and the real estate agency. Taking all this into consideration, it probably is *not* advisable for you to reveal to your agent exactly how low you are willing to go in order to sell your home.

Obviously, as the above indicates, self-interest motivates agents, and this does not necessarily always coincide with getting you the highest price. The longer your house is on the market, the more money the agent must spend on advertising and overhead, and the more time he or she must give to showing the house. The agent's additional profit in selling your home at a higher price is only a small percentage of the difference between the price you want and the price the buyer is offering. That amount might not compensate the agent for the extra time and trouble. So the agent has some incentive to close the deal and collect the commission.

In addition to advising you on counteroffer and negotiating strategy and giving you feedback on buyer reaction and mood, the real estate agent acts as the liaison between you and the buyer (or between your attorney and the buyer's attorney). Offers and counteroffers are communicated (preferably in writing) via the agent, rather than over the phone or face-to-face between you and the buyer. This eliminates subjective and emotional reactions and potential arguments or misunderstandings.

Do not get offended if the agent brings you offers you think are insultingly low. In all likelihood, your agent warned the buyer that the offer would be rejected. Nevertheless, the agent is required to communicate all real offers to you.

CONTINGENCIES AND CONDITIONS

Typically an offer made on a property consists of two parts: the price and the contingencies or conditions. A *contingency* is a special condition attached to the terms of sale; if the condition is not met, the parties are released from the contract and the sale does not go through. Contingencies are of two types. Some are conditions or concessions that make the net price of the property higher or lower to the buyer.

Example: You have an offer for your house of $140,000, with the condition that the electrical service is to be upgraded from 60 to 200 amps. The cost of the upgrade is $2,500. Since this must come out of your pocket, the net to you is $137,500 ($140,000 − $2,500). That means a second buyer offering $139,000 with *no* conditions is actually making a better offer.

The second type of contingency doesn't cost you money, but could cost you the sale—that is, the contract may be canceled if the conditions of the contingency clause are not met.

Example: Your home is in an area known to have high levels of radon. The buyer makes an offer contingent on a satisfactory radon inspection. If high levels of radon are found, the buyer can cancel the contract with no penalty.

Contingencies or conditions that govern an offer and contract are not preset, but are negotiated as part of the selling package. A buyer might offer to buy your house for a given amount, provided you repair the sidewalk before he or she moves in, for example. That's a reasonable request if the sidewalk is a shambles. But you don't have to agree to it. The buyer may make a counteroffer and walk away, or accept your offer and handle the sidewalk repair himself or herself.

How flexible you should be about contingencies depends on whether you're in a seller's market or a buyer's market, on the condition of your property, on the price you want to get, on how eager you are to sell, and on the quality and quantity of the offers you are getting.

Once contingencies are negotiated, they become part of the deal and are written into your contract.

Here are the most common conditions and contingencies:

Home Repair.   Items that buyers frequently want fixed include appliances, holes in walls or ceilings, a wet basement, a leaky roof, bad plumbing or inadequate wiring, and air conditioners.

Your buyer's lender might also want some repairs done before closing. Fixing the problems is not negotiable in such a case, but who pays for them is. If you want to make a concession to clinch the sale, you can either pay for the repair yourself or lower the price of the house. Or you and the buyer can share the cost.

Often buyers use the results of a home inspection as a negotiating tool. They note that your roof has a leak and suggest that you lower the price $3,000 to compensate, for example. A good counterstrategy is to get a written estimate from a qualified contractor of your choice for making the repair. That way, you can set the repair price yourself.

Termites.   Depending on state regulations and the lender's requirements, you may be required to have a termite inspection. If termites are found, you will have to have the house treated before the closing. Termite extermination can range from $300 to $500, depending on the level of infestation and the size of the house. Since termites can do major structural damage, it's recommended that you check for termites yourself if you have not had an inspection within the past ten years.

Radon.   Since prolonged exposure to high levels of radon can be harmful to health, many buyers insist that a sale be contingent on a radon inspection.

Radon tests range from between $10 and $20 for a do-it-yourself test to $100 or more for professional inspection. Home tests may take a slightly longer time to produce results, whereas professional tests work more quickly.

If high levels of radon are found, systems can be installed to correct the problem; the cost ranges from $2,000 to $2,500 or more.

Asbestos.   Inhaled asbestos particles become permanently lodged in the lungs and can cause serious or even fatal illness. Asbestos is found primarily in old homes, where it was once used to insulate pipes or as part of floor tiles.

If a home inspection reveals asbestos, buyers may make the sale contingent on its removal. This must be done by a qualified asbestos removal company, and can be risky because the removal process can actually release particles into the air where there were none before. The firm's fee should be contingent on a reading showing no asbestos in the air, based on a test done by a lab not connected with the contractor. The removal firm should be bonded and carry liability insurance.

Home Inspection. Most home sales are contingent on a satisfactory home inspection. If the inspection reveals defects, the buyer is not obliged to go forward with the deal until the problems have been resolved. You should try to persuade the buyer to inspect the home immediately after the accepted offer, *before* going to contract.

Sale of Existing Home. From your point of view, this is an undesirable contingency. You risk taking your home off the market only to have the buyer cancel the sale because of failure to get the asking price for his or her home.

Financing. The sale is typically contingent on the buyer obtaining financing. This is one contingency that cannot be negotiated; the buyer can't pay you if the bank won't give him or her a mortgage. One way to avoid delays or lost sales is to require serious buyers to have a letter of prequalification from a lender.

Title. The sale is usually contingent on your having clear title to the property.

OFFER AND COUNTEROFFER STRATEGY

Negotiations begin when the buyer gives you an offer, usually in writing. The offer is presented in a contract or offer form indicating the offering price, the amount of the down payment, the amount of the mortgage, the proposed closing date, and a list of items to

WHAT'S INCLUDED?

Another issue subject to negotiation is what comes with the house and what does not.

Items that can either be included with the house or taken with you include furniture, carpets, window treatments, chandeliers and other custom lighting fixtures, stoves, ovens, refrigerators, washer/dryers, humidifiers, window air conditioners, swing sets, above-ground swimming pools, garage-door openers—almost anything that's not bolted down or part of the structure.

These items should not be major points of disagreement, but whether or not an item is left in place can be used to close a deal. If you and the buyer are at an impasse, you can offer to throw in the washer/dryer, the freezer in the basement, or the French chandelier in the dining room. Many stalled negotiations have been successfully concluded because the seller ultimately "sweetened" the deal in this manner.

be included with the property. The offer is usually accompanied by a small deposit or earnest-money check—typically $1,000 or 1 percent of the price.

When you get the buyer's first offer, don't react instantly. Think about it, in privacy. Evaluate the offer with respect to your needs, your feelings, the market, and perhaps in comparison with other offers. Then respond to the offer. Your options include accepting or rejecting it outright, or making a counteroffer.

Many people believe that the first offer should be rejected automatically on the grounds that the buyer *never* offers the maximum he or she is prepared to pay. This may or may not be true. In fact, the offer may be right on the mark—the seller may have been lucky enough to find early on a buyer whose needs, tastes, and budget match the home. So evaluate all offers objectively. By rejecting the first good offer, you risk losing it, and there may not be another for some time to come.

What type of first offer can you expect? A serious offer in a normal to hot market should be around 10 percent below your asking price. On a $200,000 home, that is about $180,000. In a slow market, the first offer from a serious buyer is probably somewhere between 15 or 20 percent below your asking price.

In a seller's market, you might reject any offer below your listing price if you think your home is reasonably priced, or your counteroffer will be closer to your listing price than it would be in a buyer's market. If you deliberately priced high, you might accept an offer close but not equal to the asking price.

In a buyer's market, there is an oversupply of available houses. The buyer who offers 15 or 20 percent below your asking price is serious and is looking for a counteroffer. A buyer who offers 30 to 50 percent below your asking price is looking for a distressed, desperate seller. If you aren't in this category, pass on this offer.

ACCEPTING THE OFFER

You and the buyer have come to an agreement when you have settled on these points:

- □ the exact amount the buyer will pay you for the house
- □ the specific household items and appliances to be included in the sale and those that are not included
- □ the contingencies to be written into the contract
- □ the closing date (when title transfers from you to the buyers)
- □ the buyer occupancy date, which is often—but not always—the closing date

This final offer must be in writing and follow the laws of your state. Hire a real estate attorney to draw up the offer as a legally binding contract.

13

Making
a Contract

The contract of sale (or purchase agreement) describes in precise legal terms the property you are selling, how much you will be paid for it, and when the transfer of money and deed is to occur. It also explains the obligations of the seller and the buyer, and contains contingencies that allow either party to back out of the transaction.

Although it may be the practice in your area to use standardized, fill-in-the-blanks forms when preparing a contract, there is really no such thing as a "standard" real estate deal. Contracts are almost always modified to reflect the concerns of the parties involved. Laws governing real estate transactions also differ from state to state, and even from one county to the next. Given all of these variables, protect your interests by enlisting the services of an attorney experienced in real estate transactions. Also, relative to the value of the home, the protections afforded by an attorney are very worthwhile.

CHOOSING A LAWYER

Select your attorney carefully, because the lawyer's style and experience, or lack of them, can affect the outcome of the sale. An attorney who takes an adversarial posture during negotiations may not be skilled in the fine art of compromise, which is essential in real estate matters. At the same time, you don't want to be represented by someone who is complacent and careless and who fails to protect your interests.

To find an attorney, ask other homeowners, lenders, or corporate relocation departments for their recommendations. A real estate agent can also be a good source, provided he or she recommends more than one attorney. If a broker suggests only one name, the real client is probably the real estate agent, and the lawyer may be hesitant to challenge the agent for fear of losing referrals.

After you've identified several candidates, call the local bar association to see whether there are any ethics violations against them. Next, arrange an interview with each lawyer. You can make the initial contact by phone. Explain your purpose, and then schedule an appointment. Under these circumstances, most attorneys won't charge for the initial interview, provided you don't ask for advice about specific problems. Ask the attorney the following questions:

- ☐ How much do you charge?
- ☐ Under what conditions might you increase your fee?
- ☐ If the deal falls through, how much do you charge?
- ☐ Will you put the fee agreement in writing?
- ☐ How many closings do you handle in this state each year?
- ☐ Who covers for you if you can't attend the closing?
- ☐ Do you have paralegals working for you?
- ☐ How many years' experience do you have in residential real estate?
- ☐ May I contact previous clients?

☐   Are you covered by malpractice insurance?
☐   May I contact you after business hours?

Although the fee is an important consideration—particularly if you're trying to hold down your expenses—it shouldn't be the deciding factor. A lawyer who charges a fee that is substantially lower than others' may not put a lot of work into your case. At the same time, you probably don't need the state's leading real estate attorney, whose fees may be as impressive as his or her reputation. Furthermore, fees are not regulated, so they vary widely. Find out exactly what services you're getting for your money.

Your lawyer should have a concentration in real estate and at least five years' experience in the field. Real estate attorneys understand the value of compromise and the need to keep things moving quickly. And an experienced lawyer has knowledge that can save clients money.

A lawyer who is unfamiliar with real estate practices in your state may get caught up in arguments over procedure rather than substantive contract issues. If your attorney is licensed to practice in more than one state, make sure he or she does a substantial number of closings—about 30—in your state each year.

Although you want your lawyer to be thorough, avoid an attorney who is excessively pedantic and concerned with trifles; he or she can slow the selling process and frustrate the other parties in the deal.

A lawyer whose staff includes paralegals can delegate much of the paperwork to the assistants and concentrate on larger issues. As a bonus, the process may go faster and the fee may be lower.

Make sure your lawyer has time to represent you. You don't want to be pushed aside because your attorney is preparing a major case in court. If your lawyer can't attend the closing, make sure the substitute attorney knows the details of your transaction and will represent you effectively.

Most important, select a lawyer with whom you are comfortable *before* you have an accepted offer. There's no time to do much looking when you need an immediate contract.

THE CONTRACT

Typically, contracts are written by either a broker or a lawyer. If you sell your home yourself, you can write your own contract with the help of a standardized form, but always send the contract to a lawyer for review. Another approach is to give the information you want included in the contract to an attorney, who then will draft the legal document. In almost every state, a real estate contract *must* be in writing to be enforceable.

Contracts prepared by brokers tend to favor sellers because real estate agents are bound legally to get the best price and terms possible for their clients. At the same time, brokers also want to protect their interests. As a result, your buyer's attorney may be on the lookout for clauses that seem too protective of the seller or broker or too burdensome for the buyer.

Although no two contracts are alike, certain elements are included in every one:

Date.   To be a legal instrument, the contract must be dated.

Identities and Current Addresses of Seller(s) and Buyer(s).
Use the full, legal name of all parties involved—John J. Smith and Mary L. Smith, husband and wife, rather than Mr. and Mrs. John Smith.

Address of the Property.   The street address is usually sufficient. You might, however, want to use a more specific identification that includes the municipal tax map's block and lot numbers. A "metes and bounds" description is the safest and best.

Purchase Price and Manner of Payment.   Include the amount of the initial deposit, the amount of an additional deposit payable after the contract has been signed by both parties, the date when that additional payment is due, the amount of the mortgage, and the balance due at the closing.

Designation of Escrow Agent.   Any money that is paid out before all terms of the contract are met is kept in a special account, or *escrow fund*. The party responsible for the escrow fund can be a lawyer, lender, title company, or escrow company. Brokers can also be escrow agents, but some buyers are uncomfortable with this arrangement because the broker is not a neutral party to the deal. For the same reason, a buyer might object to the seller's attorney acting as the escrow agent.

If the money is to be held in an interest-bearing account, the contract specifies who gets the interest (buyer or seller, or a split) and who receives the money (and when) if the sale doesn't close.

Time and Date of Closing.   How you phrase this can be critical if you need to close by a certain date. If the contract says the closing will occur "on or about" June 30, legally there's no violation of the contract's terms if your buyer isn't ready to close by that time.

To ensure that you close on the date you want, include the phrase "time is of the essence," which means the closing must occur on the specified date. You can even write in that if the closing doesn't occur by then, the buyers lose their earnest-money deposit. This doesn't mean you can't agree to a new closing date later. But such a clause protects you from having to stand idly by, losing other selling opportunities, if the buyers don't meet the specified closing date.

If closing by a certain date isn't crucial to you, the date and time are likely to change. When you draw up the contract, it's impossible to know everyone's schedule months in the future. The closing can be moved to another time or place by mutual agreement of the parties.

Type of Deed.   One of the most important elements in any real estate transaction is the *deed*, the instrument used to convey title from one party to another. Depending on where you live, different types of deeds are used for this purpose. Some deeds make guarantees regarding previous owners; avoid such a deed and stick to promises of delivering a clear title only as far as your own acts as owner are concerned. Check with your lawyer if you don't know which type of deed is being used.

Personal Property. This covers removable items such as carpeting, appliances, ceiling fans, light fixtures, closet organizers, and window blinds. The contract should indicate precisely what remains with the house and what goes with you.

Condition of the Property. Usually the buyer agrees to accept the property "as is," unless you have guaranteed to make some repairs or improvements. You are responsible for routine maintenance until the buyer takes possession.

Completion of Work. If you are currently doing work on your home—for example, repainting the exterior or adding a room—the contract may stipulate that the work must be finished before the closing.

Other standard clauses include who pays the various closing costs (usually the buyer); how the responsibility for payment of taxes, utilities, heating oil, and other periodic expenses is divided between seller and buyer; the buyer's right to inspect the property before closing; liability for property loss or damage prior to the closing (usually it's the seller's responsibility, but this is specified); and the amount of the real estate commission (use an exact number, not a percentage) and to whom it is paid.

If you're selling a co-op or condo, your contract may have to include additional provisions or documentation. Your lawyer should be familiar with these items. Also check with your co-op corporation or condo association about its procedures for selling and requirements for prospective buyers. Many co-ops require buyers to be interviewed by the board of directors, for example.

Other Seller Clauses

Practically everything in a real estate transaction is negotiable. You can add a new clause or alter a standard one if the provisions seem out of the ordinary or burdensome to you (don't go overboard). If you have a particular worry about protecting your interests, share it with your lawyer. He or she can add a clause to the contract.

If you promised certain incentives to your buyers, these arrangements should be written into the contract, including how they are to be delivered to the buyer.

Here are some additions or alterations you might want to make to your contract:

Closing Costs. If you and the buyer have agreed to special arrangements regarding the closing costs, indicate this in the contract. The clause might say that both parties are splitting the costs equally, that the seller pays certain expenses and the buyer others, or that the seller pays all costs.

Special Financing. If you're offering financing to your buyer (see chapter 9), clearly indicate that in the terms of the contract. Specify the interest rate and any special provisions regarding payments. Attach copies of the note and mortgage to be signed at closing.

Date of Possession. Buyers usually take possession of the property at the closing. If you can't move into your new home yet, and the buyers are willing, you may be able to rent your old home from the buyers for a certain period. Similarly, the buyers may want to move in before the closing (see chapter 14). In either circumstance, the possession clause should indicate that one party will sign a residential lease agreement with the other, and specify the period during which the property will be leased, and the amount of rent.

Buyer Default Clause. This clause states that if the buyer reneges on the deal for any reason other than those described in the sales contract, you keep the deposit. Some sellers may want to retain the option to sue for damages up to the full purchase price of the home.

Similarly, the buyer might want a seller default clause, which holds you responsible for paying an amount up to double the deposit if you back out of the deal, but this clause is very rarely included.

Arbitration Clause. You and the buyer can agree to seek binding arbitration in the event that an unresolvable problem arises after the contract is signed. Binding arbitration means that both parties will abide by the arbitrator's decision. (The American Arbitrators Association provides skilled arbitrators who can work out equitable solutions.)

Other Buyer Clauses

Expect the buyer's attorney to strike certain clauses, particularly if the contract was prepared by your broker. You may have to decide whether you can live with the following changes:

Extension of the Lawyer Review Period. In your state, it may be the custom to place a limit on the time lawyers have to review the contract—usually three days or so. The buyer's attorney may request extra time to allow more discussion of the terms with your lawyer. This delay can work to your advantage. A lawyer who feels pressed for time may reject the entire contract over one objectionable clause. If the attorneys have enough time to work things out, the deal may proceed smoothly.

Elimination of the Broker's Mortgage Requirements. Some contracts require that the buyer obtain a mortgage through the broker. However, the only responsibility a buyer has to a broker is to acknowledge that he or she worked with the broker and that the seller pays the commission.

Striking of Exculpatory Clauses. An increasing number of buyers who discover problems with their new homes after the sale are successfully suing brokers on the grounds that the real estate agents misled or deceived them. To protect themselves, many brokers now add clauses advising buyers that they and their salespeople have no special training that allows them to identify or evaluate a home's physical defects. A buyer's lawyer may strike this clause to protect his or her client.

Expansion of Home Inspection Terms. A seller usually agrees to fix only structural defects that are discovered during the home inspection. Certain problems, such as a faulty furnace or broken washing machine, are not considered structural defects. The buyer may want an agreement on who pays to repair these items. Similarly, the buyer's attorney may set very specific terms governing the results of other inspections, such as the presence of asbestos on the premises, or radon levels.

Contingencies that Affect the Sale

Before a contract becomes binding, certain contingencies must be satisfied. So it's important to understand the terms of the contingencies clearly *before* you sign the contract. If these contingencies are not met, the contract is voidable and the buyer has the right to get back his or her deposit.

The major contingencies included in most real estate transactions are these:

Home Inspection. All buyers want to be sure that the physical condition of the property is good and that essential systems such as heating, electrical, and plumbing are in proper working order. An evaluation of your property by a professional home inspector will probably take place soon after you accept the buyer's offer. In fact, the contract should specify that the home inspection be performed by a certain date. If defects are found, you and the buyer can negotiate who is responsible for the repairs. Buyers often suggest that sellers lower their price in exchange for their taking care of the repairs themselves.

Termite Inspection. Inspections are almost always recommended, even if termites aren't a serious problem in your area. If signs of termites are found, the seller usually pays for extermination and damage repair. However, the buyer can also back out of the deal.

Mortgage. Obtaining a mortgage is the most important contingency of the contract, unless the buyer has the cash to pay the full purchase price. Buyers and their lawyers will insist on inclusion of mortgage contingency clauses with a specific cutoff date. If the buyer fails to obtain a mortgage within a certain period of time, the sale is off and the buyer gets back his or her deposit. Without this clause, you can keep the earnest-money deposit if the buyer cancels the deal because he or she can't get a mortgage.

Title Contingency. A title company conducts a title search, usually at the buyer's expense, to determine whether the title is free and clear of liens or encumbrances. The buyer may request that the title be "insurable" and "marketable." *Insurable* simply means that the buyer can get title insurance. However, *marketable* promises that there are no liens or encumbrances against the property.

Sale of the Current Home. Most people must sell their current homes before they can afford to purchase new ones. In some areas—California, for one—contracts routinely include a clause that the purchase is contingent on the sale of the buyer's current home. Market conditions can affect both the seller's and the buyer's feelings about this matter. In a slow market, this contingency protects the purchaser from carrying two mortgages, and the seller may acquiesce on this point because of the scarcity of buyers. However, you can give the buyer a limited time—such as 48 hours—in which to commit to the purchase if you receive another offer. In a strong market, with plenty of eager buyers, you would most likely reject this contingency.

Appraisals. This contingency allows the buyer to withdraw the offer if an appraisal shows that the property is worth less than a specific amount. Lenders appraise a property when determining whether to provide a mortgage.

Seller Payment of Escrow Fees and Title Insurance Fees. The buyer normally pays these fees, but may ask you to do so. Whether or not you agree may depend on the market, how many other demands the buyer has made, and how flexible you're willing to be.

14

Attending
the Closing

The closing is the final step of the selling process. You collect your money—although a good portion of it may go to your lender to repay the balance of your mortgage—the buyer receives the deed and the keys to the home, and the agent gets his or her commission. It may be held in one of the lawyers' offices, at the title company, or at the lender's office, among other places.

Exact procedures, documents, and the number of individuals involved in the closing vary within states, between states, and in different parts of the country, according to state laws and local customs. That is why it's important to hire a lawyer to oversee the closing and ensure that all the paperwork is completed properly. One item that is forgotten or not completed on time can delay the closing and frustrate everyone.

ROLES AND FUNCTIONS OF PERSONS PRESENT AT THE CLOSING

The seller's real estate agent, perhaps the buyer's agent, the escrow agent (if one is involved), the seller, the buyer, their attorneys, and perhaps a representative of the title insurance company and the seller's and buyer's lenders may attend the closing. Your lender may send a representative to collect payment on the balance of your mortgage. The buyer's lender may attend to provide the buyer with money to pay you.

The Agents

Your agent should keep in touch with the buyer's agent and with you to see if any problems develop with the buyer's search for a mortgage. The agent should also keep track of how you and the buyer are faring in meeting contingencies. He or she is also responsible for calling the people who are to be at the closing, to make sure they know the correct date, time, and place.

Essentially, the agent's role is to confirm that everyone is taking the proper steps to ensure a smooth closing by the date specified in the sales contract. Both agents should also help keep tabs on the necessary paperwork, although the lawyers are primarily responsible for completing all documents.

Your agent must also give you a receipt for payment of the commission, stating that you owe no further debts to the broker.

The Seller

Your primary responsibility as the seller is to show up at the closing with checks to pay your broker, attorney, lender (if there is a balance remaining on your mortgage), and the escrow agent. You will also need proof that you have paid your real estate taxes up to the date of transfer of title, and paid the transfer tax or recording tax on the real estate that is being transferred (the amount is determined by the county recorder).

Usually, you must also do the following:

☐ Make and pay for any repairs that were agreed on in the sales contract.

☐ Eliminate termites and correct and pay for any termite damage uncovered by the buyer's inspection.

☐ Resolve any problems with the title, such as paying off a contractor's lien, and produce an abstract of title or other document showing the title is clear.

☐ Notify utility and service companies that you are moving out on a specific date and that they are either to discontinue service or to read the meter on that date and then begin charging the new owner.

☐ If required by the sales contract, you must have a property survey performed, although the buyer typically pays for it.

☐ Pay any special assessments charged to your property for street repaving, sewer work, and so forth. Special assessments are normally paid over a period of time, with you paying the charges already levied and the buyer assuming payments from the time of closing. This is negotiable, however.

The Buyer

The buyer's primary role is to obtain the mortgage commitment. He or she does this by providing the lender with all the necessary information and documentation to prevent delays in the mortgage approval. Under the federal Real Estate Settlement Procedures Act (RESPA), the buyer's lender must give the buyer a list of all closing costs, documents, and services paid, assembled, or performed by the closing.

At closing, the buyer should bring certified checks as specified by you, your attorney, or the lender. He or she should also bring a checkbook to pay for expected or possibly unexpected costs. These typically include any expenses owed to the lender that have not already been paid, the title insurance premium, escrow agent's fees, lawyer's fees, survey costs (if a survey was required), and deed recording fees.

The buyer usually must also do these three things:

BEFORE YOU MOVE OUT

Buyers may ask you for specific information about your home or community. As a goodwill gesture, take the initiative and provide your buyer with additional material about the property and important community resources.

Gather the information in a folder or attractive box. The file should contain warranty information and owner's manuals for appliances in the home as well as any valid service contracts. Also include the locations of electrical panels, main water and gas valves, septic tank and leach fields, and any other vital systems. Buyers will also appreciate getting a plan of the garden, listing the types of plants, flowers, trees, and shrubbery planted on the property, along with instructions for their care. Leave a list of names and numbers of service people who are familiar with the house, too.

Other useful items are the latest bus and train timetables, schedules for garbage pickup, including recyclable materials, and emergency numbers for police, fire, and ambulance. You might also provide a profile of your community that includes data on clubs and organizations, places of worship, stores and restaurants, parks and recreational areas, and information on schools, the library, and the municipal building.

If you're selling a condo or co-op, advise your buyer about the procedures for moving in, and offer to introduce the new residents to the staff. Include information about amenities such as tennis courts, pools, or recreation areas and the policies governing their use. If your complex has laundry rooms or storage areas, note their location and the hours they are open, as well as the cost per use of washing machines and dryers. General information regarding visitor parking, security, and deliveries is also helpful.

- ☐ Pay for a homeowner's insurance policy to take effect the day title is transferred. (The buyer can assume your policy and reimburse you for the unused portion.)
- ☐ See that all other contingencies in the sales contract are met.
- ☐ Notify gas, oil, electric, water, telephone, and cable companies to connect the utilities and begin charging them to the buyer as of the date of title transfer.

The Attorneys

The buyer's and seller's attorneys are present at the closing to represent their clients and to see that any last-minute problems are resolved equitably and, if possible, in their clients' favor. They also review any documents that were not available or completed until closing.

The buyer's attorney usually chooses a title insurance company to conduct a title search and property survey. Title insurance protects the lender in case a lien or other problem with the title turns up that might make the lender responsible for unpaid debts. A buyer should also purchase title insurance to protect his or her interests.

Prior to closing, the buyer's attorney also checks the mortgage commitment and sales contract. At closing, the attorney may be representing the buyer's lender as well. In any case, the buyer's lawyer makes sure all documents required of the buyer are completed as required.

Your lawyer prepares the deed to your home for transfer to the buyer and should also remind you about the certified check due to your lender to pay off the balance on your loan. (You must call your lender and arrange to get a "pay-off letter," which states the amount that is due the lender.) Your attorney should also estimate all of the closing costs and go over them with the buyer's attorney. Both lawyers review all available closing documents before closing and review any new documents at closing. Both lawyers also help resolve any problems that may arise at the closing.

PRORATING EXPENSES

Certain costs are prorated between buyer and seller at closing, according to usage during the year. Typical prorated expenses are homeowner's insurance, if the buyer is assuming the seller's policy; real estate taxes; rental income on an investment property; and items such as heating oil that you have paid for but not used completely. Request your oil company to read the meter on your tank and give you a written statement showing how much oil is left in the fuel tank, along with how much was last delivered and its cost. This should be done the day before closing.

You need your insurance company's approval to have the buyer assume your homeowner's insurance policy, but most companies will agree to do so. You may come out ahead by transferring your policy instead of simply canceling it; the insurance company will probably not reimburse you for the full unused portion of your policy, but a buyer who prorates the cost will refund you the balance.

Your lawyer can help you determine the proration of other items.

GUARANTEEING A SMOOTH CLOSING

The best way to prevent problems occurring at the closing is to delineate carefully in the sales contract all the terms, costs, and responsibilities of both buyer and seller. You should keep in touch with your lawyer to make sure all the necessary paperwork is progressing and that each party is fulfilling his or her obligations. Your real estate agent may agree to keep both sides in the transaction informed of progress or problems, and can track the myriad tasks that need to be accomplished prior to closing.

Once at the closing, the agent and lawyers can step in to solve any last-minute obstacles or disputes. For example, if the buyer suddenly insists that an air conditioner be included as part of the deal, or that you pay for a repair, the lawyers can point out that

SHOULD YOU ALLOW THE BUYER TO TAKE POSSESSION BEFORE CLOSING?

The consensus of real estate agents and lawyers to the above question is no, unless the buyer has put down a substantial nonrefundable earnest-money deposit. Too many potential problems may occur, such as these:

- ☐ A major appliance or system could break down or a fire could break out in the house. If the home is damaged, the question of who is responsible for repairing the damage, or whose insurance company is responsible, can cause liability headaches for everyone.
- ☐ The buyer could back out of the sale because something isn't "right" with the home or neighborhood. Even a noisy toilet or uneven floorboards could prompt a dissatisfied buyer to ask for a price reduction or repair that ordinarily would not have been considered.

If you do allow possession before closing, or if the buyer agrees to let *you* stay on the premises after title is transferred, draw up a rental agreement and include a possession clause in the sales contract. The clause should state how long the rental is for, and the amount of the monthly rent.

those items were not included in the purchase agreement. Or perhaps during the walk-through of the property, which usually takes place the day before the closing, the buyer discovered that you removed a light fixture that was supposed to be included with the property, or you failed to clean out the basement or garage. In that case you might be asked to pay something extra to compensate the buyer and allow the closing to continue.

You are required to leave the home "broom-clean" if not necessarily spotless. Remember, too, that everything the contract stated was to remain in the house must remain. Any item that is attached to the home but was not specifically excluded from the sale must also be left behind.

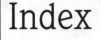

Index